D0803241

Forensic Biology

Other titles in the Crime Scene Investigations series:

Forensic Biology

by Jenny MacKay

LUCENT BOOKS
A part of Gale, Cengage Learning

GALE
CENGAGE Learning™

Detroit • New York • San Francisco • New Haven, Conn • Waterville, Maine • London

© 2009 Gale, Cengage Learning

Every effort has been made to trace the owners of copyrighted material.

LIBRARY OF CONGRESS CATALOGING-IN-PUBLICATION DATA

MacKay, Jenny, 1978-
  Forensic biology / by Jenny MacKay.
    p. cm. — (Crime scene investigations)
  Includes bibliographical references and index.
  ISBN 978-1-4205-0108-7 (hardcover)
  1. Forensic biology—Juvenile literature. I. Title.
  QH313.5.F67M33 2009
  614'.1—dc22

2008053577

Lucent Books
27500 Drake Rd
Farmington Hills MI 48331

ISBN-13: 978-1-4205-0108-7
ISBN-10: 1-4205-0108-9

Printed in the United States of America
1 2 3 4 5 6 7 13 12 11 10 09

Contents

Foreword

The popularity of crime scene and investigative crime shows on television has come as a surprise to many who work in the field. The main surprise is the concept that crime scene analysts are the true crime solvers, when in truth, it takes dozens of people, doing many different jobs, to solve a crime. Often, the crime scene analyst's contribution is a small one. One Minnesota forensic scientist says that the public "has gotten the wrong idea. Because I work in a lab similar to the ones on *CSI*, people seem to think I'm solving crimes left and right—just me and my microscope. They don't believe me when I tell them that it's just the investigators that are solving crimes, not me."

Crime scene analysts do have an important role to play, however. Science has rapidly added a whole new dimension to gathering and assessing evidence. Modern crime labs can match a hair of a murder suspect to one found on a murder victim, for example, or recover a latent fingerprint from a threatening letter, or use a powerful microscope to match tool marks made during the wiring of an explosive device to a tool in a suspect's possession.

Probably the most exciting of the forensic scientist's tools is DNA analysis. DNA can be found in just one drop of blood, a dribble of saliva on a toothbrush, or even the residue from a fingerprint. Some DNA analysis techniques enable scientists to tell with certainty, for example, whether a drop of blood on a suspect's shirt is that of a murder victim.

While these exciting techniques are now an essential part of many investigations, they cannot solve crimes alone. "DNA doesn't come with a name and address on it," says the Minnesota forensic scientist. "It's great if you have someone in custody to match the sample to, but otherwise, it doesn't help.

That's the investigator's job. We can have all the great DNA evidence in the world, and without a suspect, it will just sit on a shelf. We've all seen cases with very little forensic evidence get solved by the resourcefulness of a detective."

While forensic specialists get the most media attention today, the work of detectives still forms the core of most criminal investigations. Their job, in many ways, has changed little over the years. Most cases are still solved through the persistence and determination of a criminal detective whose work may be anything but glamorous. Many cases require routine, even mind-numbing tasks. After the July 2005 bombings in London, for example, police officers sat in front of video players watching thousands of hours of closed-circuit television tape from security cameras throughout the city, and as a result were able to get the first images of the bombers.

The Lucent Books Crime Scene Investigations series explores the variety of ways crimes are solved. Titles cover particular crimes such as murder, specific cases such as the killing of three civil rights workers in Mississippi, or the role specialists such as medical examiners play in solving crimes. Each title in the series demonstrates the ways a crime may be solved, from the various applications of forensic science and technology to the reasoning of investigators. Sidebars examine both the limits and possibilities of the new technologies and present crime statistics, career information, and step-by-step explanations of scientific and legal processes.

The Crime Scene Investigations series strives to be both informative and realistic about how members of law enforcement—criminal investigators, forensic scientists, and others—solve crimes, for it is essential that student researchers understand that crime solving is rarely quick or easy. Many factors—from a detective's dogged pursuit of one tenuous lead to a suspect's careless mistakes to sheer luck to complex calculations computed in the lab—are all part of crime solving today.

The Science of Life

Crime is often a life-and-death situation. Criminals may take a life. It is law enforcement officers' job to save one. The evidence left behind in the wake of a crime often stems from living things, and in the end, the criminal's life may be at stake if he or she is caught.

Everywhere on earth, there is life. From the plants that surround people to the organisms that live within them, the cells that compose them to the illnesses they fear, humans cannot ignore living things in their quest to solve crimes. Biology, the study of living things, is the science most intricately connected with crime fighting. Because crimes take place in the living world, scientists constantly seek new ways to use the principles of living things to solve criminal cases—even those that have ended in death.

Fields Within Forensic Biology

Today, branches of life science such as botany are being used in new and exciting ways to prove that many criminals collect plant evidence—on their car, clothing, or body—from the exact location of their crime. Plants have always been silent witnesses to crime, but modern botanists who study plant life have contributed much to criminology by showing how plants deposit evidence in many criminal cases. From seed pods dropped in a suspect's vehicle to a thin film of pollen on a suspect's clothes, plant evidence can link perpetrators to victims and to the scene of the crime. The increased admission of plant DNA as evidence in criminal cases shows how forensic botany may change the future of crime scene investigation.

Bacteria and insects, like plants, are unassuming creatures, but they usually find dead bodies much sooner than police do. Forensic microbiologists examine the growth of bacteria in a

dead body, and forensic entomologists study insect eggs and offspring on the corpse. Scientists who study flesh eaters, both the insects and the bacteria that decompose the dead, use the life cycles of these organisms to better inform the timeline of human death. Determining how long a body has been dead is the branch of forensic biology called taphonomy.

Although it is often overlooked, plant evidence collected at a crime scene can provide important clues about the case.

Anthropologists, scientists of human culture, join forces with modern dentists to transform these branches of biology into crime-solving studies. Looking closely at the bones and teeth of human remains, these forensic experts work to match the dead with the identities they had when they were alive. As counterparts to anthropologists and forensic dentists, the forensic serologists who study body fluids of both the living and the dead are developing and improving ways to compare biological fluid samples to identify offenders and close criminal cases.

Even crimes of global scale fall to forensic biologists. As the threat of bioterrorism looms around the world, forensic microbiologists use their knowledge of microscopic organisms to thwart the plans of criminals whose weapons of choice are germs no one can see. These scientists study disease outbreaks to determine whether illnesses have been caused intentionally by criminals. They are the detectives who track down evidence that germs have been used as weapons against people and help to trace biological weapons back to their source.

Biologists join forces with police departments who seek their skills and expertise in an endless variety of criminal cases. Creative and resourceful, the forensic biologists at work in the world today do not merely study life. They save it.

CHAPTER 1

A Trail of Plant Evidence

Plants are everywhere. In the country, open fields are blanketed with crops, wildflowers, and weeds. In forests, there are tangles of trees and roots. Cities have parks and common areas with grass, flowers, and trees. Front porches and apartment balconies overflow with plants in pots and containers. Because plants are abundant, they have the potential to be very useful for solving crimes. Plants, in the form of seeds, pollen, leaves, and stems, often create a trail of evidence during a crime. Plant matter from one location sticks to a suspect's or a victim's hair or clothing, then gets transported to wherever the suspect or victim goes next. Collecting this trace evidence from suspects or victims has the potential to give investigators important clues about where people have been and the amount of time that has passed since they visited the scene of a crime.

Despite its prevalence at crime scenes—particularly violent crimes such as rapes, assaults, and murders—investigators often overlook plant evidence. They are trained to notice other things about a scene, such as the position and the condition of a murder victim's body or the presence of a gun, knife, or other weapon. Looking for and collecting plant evidence may only be an afterthought, if crime scene investigators think of it at all. While crime scene technicians are busy with activities such as dusting for fingerprints and making casts of shoe impressions left in mud, a speck of pollen or a tiny piece of a crushed leaf on a victim's pants may be completely forgotten. It could, however, turn out to be the most important clue in the case.

Forensic scientist Heather Mill Coyle and her colleagues say it is common for police departments to overlook plant evidence, mainly because they do not realize it could be there.

"A large branch or clump of leaves found within a victim's palm will catch the curious eye of an investigator," they say, but not all plant material is this obvious. Important evidence could be almost invisible, such as a tiny piece of a crumbled leaf or a microscopic grain of pollen. "Only if an investigator is aware of the potential existence of that evidence," say Coyle and colleagues, "will any efforts be made to look for it."[1]

Forensic botany, the use of plant evidence to solve crimes, is useful only when investigators *do* make an effort to look carefully for this evidence and preserve it before it withers or rots. One reason plant material is so often overlooked as evidence is that most police departments do not have forensic botanists on staff who survey crime scenes. They have fingerprint technicians and blood spatter analysts, forensic photographers and detectives who interview witnesses, but forensic botany is not a standard step in every criminal investigation. If investigators think botany might help to solve a crime, they usually must collect and store the plant evidence themselves, then find a botany expert at a research laboratory or a university to identify the matter and decide whether or not it is significant in the case. Fictional CSI shows on television often give a picture of well-rounded detective teams that include experts in fields such as botany, but this is rarely the case. Analyzing forensic plant evidence generally requires investigators to go outside the police department to find a scientist who specializes in a field such as botany; therefore, many investigators either skip or ignore the process.

Although it is not the best known or most popular evidence in a criminal case, forensic botany has enormous potential for investigators who take the time to collect it. According to forensic botanist David W. Hall, Ph.D., "this evidence can place a person at or away from a crime scene, or help determine time of death or the time of a crime, or the cause of death or illness."[2] Some plant evidence is almost always stuck to a victim or a suspect, and it has the potential to serve as a valuable, indisputable link between suspect, victim, and the scene of a crime.

Evidence That Sticks

To reproduce, plants grow parts that are portable because they are stationary organisms. They take root in a patch of soil and stay there for life. A pine tree, for example, cannot uproot itself to find a mate, so instead, during reproductive season, it sends out microscopic reproductive missionaries to others of its kind. These float on the air in search of fellow pine trees to mate with, coating everything in their path with a fine dust called pollen. Pollen, in turn, can become valuable evidence, placing a criminal at a crime scene.

Pine trees are not alone in having a mobile method of reproduction. Most plants have portable reproductive parts. Some open fragrant flowers and entice insects to pollinate them. Some plants grow sweet fruit so that animals come along, feast, and then move elsewhere to drop the digested seeds, so a new plant can take root. Some plants release seeds in the shape of tiny propellers or with feather-like hairs to

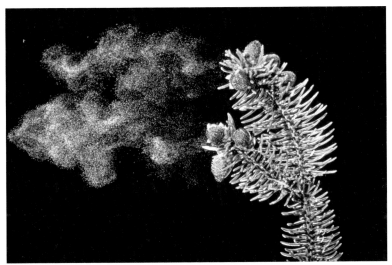

Pollen emitted from a pine tree into the air as part of the plant's reproductive process also may stick to a person's clothes and other possessions, providing evidence of where that person has been.

13

catch the wind and travel somewhere else. Others grow thorny or sticky seeds that cling to passing animals and hitchhike to a new location.

A person is as likely to transport plant matter as is any other creature that brushes against plants or walks through a cloud of microscopic pollen. Because plants are everywhere, people are always picking up bits and pieces of them: in their hair and eyelashes, on their clothing, even in their earwax. Criminals, especially, are likely to spend time in close contact with plants. They may use trees or shrubs for cover as they stalk a victim or watch a store they would like to rob. They may brush against shrubs as they assault someone in a park or field. They may disturb vegetation as they drag a victim along the ground, or they may uproot grass or small plants as they attempt to bury a body. Pollen, seeds, leaves, and broken stems get lodged in pockets and in pant cuffs, on shoelaces, and in the seams of sweatshirts and jeans. And just as investigators often underestimate the potential evidence plants may provide, criminals rarely think about plant material. They might wipe down surfaces of objects to get rid of fingerprints and they may go to great lengths to cover their footprints and tire tracks, but they are not likely to spend much time plucking thorns from their victim's pants or digging pieces of crushed leaves out of their own jacket seams.

This overlooked evidence can be an important link between a victim, a suspect, and the scene or scenes of a crime. Coyle and colleagues describe one case in which a man was discovered hanging by his neck from a tree. Investigators were unsure whether he had hung himself to commit suicide or someone else had done the hanging, but the answer eventually came from plant evidence. Moss smears on the insides of the man's wrists matched the moss on the tree from which he hung. "He must have transferred the samples to his skin while tying the rope to an upper branch," the authors say. "His death was determined to be a suicide."[3] Had investigators not found the smears of moss, they might have come to the wrong conclusion and ruled the death a murder.

Plant evidence can also provide important clues about what happened in a case of foul play, and it may even prove that a suspect is lying. Coyle and colleagues describe a case in which a man claimed he came home and found his wife, who had suffered a head injury inflicted by a blunt object, dead on the couch. When investigators examined the woman's clothing, however, they discovered bits of broken plant material that matched the plants in the couple's driveway. This suggested that the body may have been dragged up the driveway, so they considered the possibility that the injury had occurred outside, not on the couch as the husband had claimed.

Next to the pond behind the couple's house, investigators found the murder weapon—a brick with the woman's blood and hair on it. But the final clue they needed was an algae stain on the T-shirt the husband was wearing when he said he found his wife's body. "Microscopic analyses by botanists and forensic

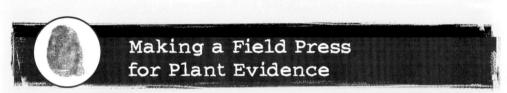

Making a Field Press for Plant Evidence

Plant material collected at crime scenes must be transported to a botanist's laboratory. To prevent these organic parts from rotting before they can be analyzed, plant evidence must be kept dry and protected. Plant materials are never put into plastic bags or containers, because these trap moisture and speed up decomposition. Instead, investigators can fashion a makeshift field press for this purpose, using a stack of folded newspaper and two pieces of cardboard cut to the same size as the folded paper. As leaves, stems, flowers, and other plant materials are collected at the crime scene, they are tucked between separate layers of newspaper. When the field press is complete, the newspaper is stacked and capped on the top and bottom with the pieces of cardboard. Then the whole package is secured with rope or string so that it can be easily carried to a botany lab. The plant evidence stays dry and safe until a botanist can analyze it.

scientists identified the algal species on the shirt as being the same as those found in the pond, thereby establishing the link between the husband and the weapon,"[4] say Coyle and colleagues. In this case, plants served one of their most important functions in forensic science: linking victims and killers to the scene of a murder.

Weeding-Out Locations

The type of plant matter present on a victim or a suspect can be proof that the person was recently in a certain location or type of environment. Like any living thing, plants have a habitat—a place with the right conditions for them to grow, reproduce, and survive. Earth has many different habitats, and plants can grow in most of them. Specific habitats, however, typically have specific types of plants. A swamp in Florida contains plants that thrive in wet, warm conditions, whereas the Arizona desert supports plants such as cacti which live in extreme heat with very little water. The grasses that grow well on the Great Plains have a much different habitat than the redwood trees towering over the hillsides of central California.

In forensic botany, different types of plants and different plant habitats can be important clues about where a crime took place. Some plants, such as weeds, are very hardy and common, and they grow almost everywhere. But other plants grow only in specific environments. Often, the most helpful plant evidence in a criminal case is evidence that a botanist links to a rare plant, one that only grows in a few particular locations. For instance, if pieces from a plant such as neoparrya, which grows only in crevices of volcanic rock in Colorado, are found on a murder victim, the evidence may indicate that the victim spent time on Colorado's volcanic rock before, during, or after her death. Such plant evidence helps investigators narrow their search for a murder scene. It could also prove that the main suspect in the murder is lying if he says he has never been near any place where neoparrya grows, but a piece of neoparrya is later found on his clothes.

The Mystery of Rail 16

In 1932 the infant son of the famous aviator Charles Lindbergh was kidnapped from his upstairs nursery. A wooden ladder was found at the scene of the crime, a handmade device with a suspicious rung at the top that did not match the others. The rung came to be known as Rail 16. When investigators searched the attic of their top suspect, Bruno Richard Hauptmann, they found a missing section of attic floorboard that looked to be about the same width and length as Rail 16. Comparisons of the two wood samples showed they were both southern yellow pine of exactly the same thickness. When the cut end of the attic floorboard was lined up with Rail 16, the marks of the wood grain aligned perfectly. The similarities proved that the ladder from the crime scene had been repaired with wood from Hauptmann's attic, thus placing him at the scene of the crime. Modern tests performed on the two wood samples have resulted in the same conclusion. Hauptmann was convicted of the kidnapping and murder of Baby Lindbergh, in part on the strength of Rail 16.

A ladder used in the 1932 Lindbergh kidnapping rests near the window of the child's nursery. Analysis of one of the ladder's rungs provided evidence that helped convict Richard Hauptmann of the crime.

In general, the rarer the plant, the more useful the evidence. When a botanist identifies plant matter from a species that grows only in a very specific place, investigators know exactly where to begin looking for additional clues in the crime. Many plants, however, grow in fairly wide habitats; they appear in all places with the right soil, temperatures, wind, moisture, and altitude. A common plant called creeping boxwood, for instance, grows almost anywhere except riverbanks and other wet locations. Despite the fact that it is much more common than neoparrya, creeping boxwood can still be useful in criminal cases. For example, if a botanist identifies creeping boxwood collected from a fisherman whose body was found floating in a swamp, the botanist will realize that the man was somewhere dry before he ended up in the swamp. Police may have been ready to rule the death a drowning accident, but the botanist's findings of a strictly dry-soil plant on the victim's remains will suggest there is more to the story.

Signs of a Season

Plant evidence helps investigators establish not just the location of a crime, but a timeline as to when it took place. Just as plants live in particular habitats, they also have certain growing seasons. Evergreen trees, for instance, release pollen when conditions are best for reproduction—usually in the cool, moist days of spring. Most grasses wait until summer to release their pollen, while most weeds pollinate in the fall. If pollen is discovered at a crime scene, therefore, identifying the type of plant it came from can provide a useful clue about what time of year the crime took place. A botanist who identifies ragweed pollen on a murder victim's clothing may deduce that the body was outdoors in the late summer or fall, when ragweed pollinates. This might help investigators narrow down the time of death, at least to the right season.

There are other seasonal clues a botanist can use to determine how long a murder victim's body has been outdoors. Botanists can usually match seeds, flowers, or berries to plant species, for instance. The presence of such items on a victim's body indicates that the victim was outdoors during the season

Ragweed pollinates in late summer and early fall, providing investigators with a seasonal clue if its pollen is discovered at a crime scene.

when the species reached that part of its growth cycle. Once they identify the plant species, botanists look up the plant's growing and reproducing patterns to give police an approximate time of the year when the victim had to have been outdoors. Botanists also can tell police where the plant grows and, therefore, where the victim must have spent time.

Planting Suspects at a Crime Scene

Pollen and seeds can be important clues not just for establishing how long a body has been lying in a forest but for linking criminals to the scenes of their crimes. Pollen, in particular, hovers in the air and collects, as a fine layer of dust, on everything in the area. Not only will a murder victim's body likely be covered with a film of pollen, but a layer of pollen also may collect on the murderer as he discards the body. The pollen and seeds of some trees and plants do not disperse well in the air, so they stay very close to their parent plant. A suspect found to have this kind of pollen or seed on his clothing, car, or other belongings can be linked to the area or perhaps even the specific tree where the crime occurred.

In her book *Forensic Botany*, Coyle describes such a case, which occurred in New Zealand. Traces of pollen were collected from the clothing of a murder victim whose body was found in the mountains outside the city of Wellington. The police had a suspect in the case, and when they searched his belongings,

Pollen covers the hood of a car parked near an oak tree. Pollen can produce evidence of a crime's timing and location.

they found traces of the same pollen on a jacket he owned. "When confronted with this evidence," Coyle says, the suspect "asserted that he had purchased the Fairydown jacket overseas, and that he had never worn it outside the Wellington metropolitan area."[5] Coyle says pollen analysis of the jacket "identified a number of pollen types including silver beech, which suggested the jacket had been out of the Wellington city limits into a mountainous area where silver beech can be found."[6] In this case, plant evidence caught the killer in his own lie—if there

By the Numbers

2 TO 4 INCHES

Depth of soil that should be removed in each layer of a forensic excavation of a body.

was silver beech pollen on his jacket, the jacket *must* have been worn in the mountains, the only place where this kind of tree grows. Investigators could prove that the jacket had traveled into the mountains outside Wellington, despite the suspect's claim that his jacket had never been worn outside the city, because silver beech trees do not grow within Wellington. Plant evidence provided an important link between this suspect and the mountains where the murder victim was found. In part because of this evidence, police were able to arrest the man for murder.

Hidden Evidence Unearthed

Sometimes, criminals unintentionally bury plant evidence that later helps investigators to solve the case. Murderers often try to cover up their crimes by hiding the evidence underground. They dig graves for the body and sometimes for the weapon, in the hope that the burial site will never be discovered. Plant evidence can be very useful in cases in which victims have been buried. Murderers who dig graves are usually so concerned with getting the body into the ground that they pay little attention to the plant matter that goes in with it. They may unknowingly be burying pollen, seeds, or other plant evidence along with the body, clues that later could pinpoint the season

Investigators collect evidence, including clues provided by plant material, from a shallow grave in an Indiana cornfield where a body was discovered in 2005.

during which the body was buried and could even link the killer to the burial site if police find the same seeds or pollen on his belongings.

Plant evidence is not important to a case if it is never found, and the killer hopes that the grave will never be discovered. But whenever a hole is dug in the earth, plants are disturbed. A grave-sized patch of land that is bare of grasses and weeds could draw attention to the burial site in the first place. Once a grave has been discovered, crime scene investigators dig it up carefully, searching for clues and evidence in the layers of dirt on top of the victim. Pieces of broken or uprooted plants, as well as layers of seeds and leaves, can give investigators important details if they take the time to collect and preserve this evidence.

"Bodies found lying on the ground are usually in areas that are abundant with plant life,"[7] says Vernon G. Geberth, a nationally renowned expert on death investigations. "When a grave is dug," he explains, "excavated soil is placed on the surface."[8] When the killer refills the grave, vegetation that was growing on the surface is often placed back into the hole. "Furthermore," says Geberth, "if the body has been buried for some time, roots of trees or bushes may grow through the remains."[9] When the grave is excavated, a professional botanist can tell investigators how long it has been since the surface vegetation was uprooted, as well as how long it would take roots from those plants to grow through the victim's remains. "Although this information will not provide an estimate of time of death," Geberth says, "it can contribute a relevant time factor to the investigation."[10]

Plant evidence helps narrow down a general time of burial, in part because plants leave layers of debris behind every year. They may flower or pollinate in the spring, and these materials fall to the ground during the summer. In the fall, some plants die, and others lose their leaves or shed their needles. In the spring, the process begins again. Police investigating a buried body, therefore, should pay attention to how many layers of dead flowers, seeds, and leaves they find covering the body to help determine how many seasons or years the victim has been in the ground.

A case of a mass burial site that was discovered in Germany in 1994 demonstrates the usefulness of taking the time to search for plant evidence. The grave contained the bodies of thirty-two men who had been buried for about four decades. Investigators concluded there were two possible events in which the men could have died. The first theory was that they were victims of the Gestapo, the Nazi police force, and that they had been killed after World War II in the spring of 1945. The second theory was that they were Soviet soldiers who had been killed during a German revolt in the summer of 1953. To solve the mystery, scientists collected pollen from the nose cavities of the victims in the grave, pollen they would have breathed in shortly before their death. "Seven of the tested skulls contained high amounts of plantain, rye, and lime tree pollen—all common for plants that flower in the summer months,"[11] say Coyle and colleagues. Thus, plant evidence showed that the men probably died in the revolt in the summer of 1953, and not in the spring of 1945.

This case shows the usefulness of plant evidence in pinpointing a season of death, even for bodies that have been buried for many years. But when police need to know a more specific time of death for a person who recently died, their investigation may broaden to include other scientists who specialize in living organisms. These are the scientists who study bacteria and insects responsible for a body's systematic decomposition. These people often can establish a much more precise time of death.

Death's Timeline

The investigation of any crime seeks answers to solve a mystery. "At every crime scene many questions are asked," says forensic anthropologist Arpad A. Vass, "but to solve the crime the five *W*'s (who, what, when, where and why) must be answered."[12] For murder investigations, establishing when the homicide took place can be crucial. Knowing the time of death can eliminate suspects from the list of people who could have committed the crime. If a suspect has an alibi (proof that he or she was somewhere else when the victim was killed), knowing the precise time of death can show that the suspect is innocent. The time of death also can destroy an alibi: a suspect who claims he was at a ball game the evening of the murder will have no alibi if investigators can prove the victim died two hours after the ball game ended.

Time of death is so important in a murder investigation that several fields of forensic science specialize in it. Collectively they are known as the studies of taphonomy, the way human bodies decompose and how long it takes them to do so. All bodies begin to break down soon after death; their tissues rot from both the inside and the outside. "Human decomposition begins approximately 4 minutes after death has occurred," says Vass, and continues until the parts of the body return "to their simplest building blocks—essentially dust to dust."[13] The branches of biology that focus on how this decomposition happens and how long it takes include forensic pathology, bacteriology, and entomology.

The Study of Human Death

Pathologists are biologists who specialize in the effect of diseases and health problems on the body's tissues. Forensic pathologists

A forensic pathologist prepares to perform an autopsy examination, which will provide information on the time and cause of death.

generally specialize in fatal injuries and death, analyzing what happens to a body when the heart no longer pumps and all living systems shut down. An important question forensic pathologists try to answer is how long ago a victim died, but environmental conditions such as temperature can affect the amount of time it takes for individual body tissues to perish after the heart stops beating. Pinpointing the exact moment a murder took place can be difficult as Colin Evans author of *Murder Two: The Second Casebook of Forensic Detection points out*. "Nothing in forensic science is trickier—or has been the cause of more bitter disputes—than the problem of establishing the time of death. It is a fiendishly difficult business, made harder still with each passing hour that the body remains unfound."[14]

Death happens at the instant the heart no longer beats and the lungs no longer breathe. All body systems shut down.

Blood pools in the veins. The cells of organs and tissues die too, and body tissues change shape, color, and texture. The immune system no longer patrols the body with germ-killing, white blood cells to keep bacteria from taking over, and bacteria soon multiply and devour everything they touch. These processes are part of decomposition. Forensic pathologists try to determine, based on how death has affected a body and on how much the body has decomposed, the amount of time the person has been dead. This can be a crucial estimate for investigators as they track down a murderer, especially one who claims to have an alibi.

When Blood Settles

As soon as the heart stops pumping, blood stops moving. Gravity pulls the blood pooled in the arteries and veins to the lowest points in the body. If a woman dies while lying on her back, her blood will sink toward the back of her torso, head,

A forensic pathologist examines a body in which livor mortis, or the reddening of tissue caused by the pooling of blood, has occurred around the shoulders.

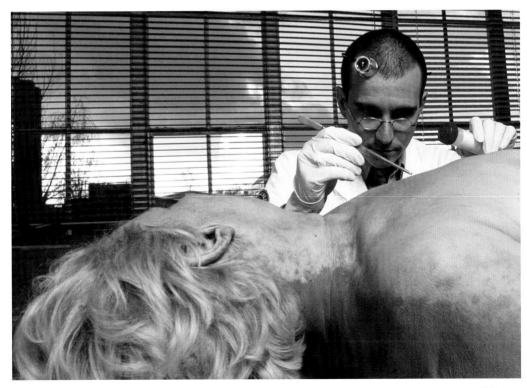

By the Numbers

30 MINUTES

Average amount of time it takes for livor mortis to begin after death.

arms, and legs. The blood collecting in these areas turns them reddish purple. This discoloration of a corpse is called livor mortis.

The collection of blood to the lowest part of a body usually begins between thirty minutes and two hours after the heart stops beating. If a dead person is moved before livor mortis is complete, the blood will change direction, but after eight to twelve hours, the blood will no longer shift. At this point, livor mortis is fixed. Because livor mortis becomes fixed within eight to twelve hours after death, it gives pathologists a rough time frame of when the victim died. Livor mortis does not, however, provide a precise measurement of time of death. Pathologists cannot use livor mortis to determine whether a victim died at 2:30 in the morning or at exactly 3:15.

Livor mortis also differs from one person and one environment to the next. The bodies of large victims may require more time for livor mortis to become fixed, because larger bodies contain more blood, and, therefore, more time must pass for all of the blood to collect at the point of lowest gravity. The process of livor mortis also might take longer in a very cold environment than a warm one because blood, like any liquid, gets slushy as it freezes. Thus it takes much more time to pool in the body's veins. Just the same, livor mortis often is used to narrow down the time of death to a twelve-hour period. It can tell investigators whether the victim died in morning or in the evening of the previous day, for example, so pathologists often consider livor mortis along with another measure of time of death—the stiffening of dead muscles, a phenomenon called *rigor mortis*.

When Corpses Stiffen

The body's muscles are powered by adenosine triphosphate, or ATP, a substance produced by the body's cells to give them energy. Muscles require a lot of ATP to do the work of

moving the body as it runs, walks, writes letters, or does any other activity. The heart, too, is a muscle, and it uses ATP to keep beating. When the body dies, its cells also begin to die, and they no longer produce the ATP that muscles need. Without ATP, muscle tissue loses its flexibility and gets stiff. The entire body, in fact, stiffens into the exact position in which it was lying after death. A stiff body is in rigor mortis.

According to Evans, rigor mortis, or the stiffening of dead muscle tissue, "usually begins to show three hours after death in the muscles of the face and eyelids, and then spreads slowly through the body to the arms and legs."[15] Typically, within six to twelve hours, the body is in complete rigor mortis and will stay in the same position even if moved. If the person died sitting in a chair, for example, rigor mortis locks the body into a

A victim's arm, rigid from rigor mortis, hovers over an examination table. The state of rigor mortis can provide evidence of time of death.

sitting position: even if the victim is moved to the floor, the legs will still be bent as if sitting in a chair. Victims of self-inflicted gunshot wounds have even been found still clutching the gun stiffly in their hand because rigor mortis set in by the time the body is discovered.

Like livor mortis, rigor mortis can give investigators a rough estimate of the time of death. It narrows down the possible time of the murder to a period of six to twelve hours, perhaps giving the pathologist an idea as to whether the victim was killed on a Tuesday evening or a Wednesday morning. Rigor mortis also can be unpredictable. In some victims, rigor mortis sets in very rapidly, much sooner than the standard six to twelve hours after death. It sets in faster in victims who were running at the time of their death, for instance, because their muscles were using ATP rapidly at that moment, so at the instant they died little ATP remained in the muscles to keep the body from getting almost instantly stiff.

"Such a wealth of variables has led some medical examiners to entirely discount rigor mortis as a means of estimating the time of death,"[16] says Evans. However, he adds, "for others it remains an invaluable if highly contentious tool."[17] After all, nearly every dead body goes through a period of rigor mortis. Only in very rare cases, such as a starved victim who had little muscle mass at the moment of death, is rigor mortis too weak to be noticeable. Although the phenomenon of rigor mortis may not be reliable in pinpointing time of death, most pathologists and investigators take it into consideration, along with other evidence they collect to estimate time of death.

For every body, the period of rigor mortis ends. After a certain amount of time passes, the muscles loosen up again. This is a sign that another process has begun in the muscles and throughout body, a process that may be even more useful in determining the length of time a body has been lifeless: the breakdown of muscles and other body tissue by bacteria.

Dead Man's Float

Murderers sometimes try to conceal their victims' bodies in lakes, rivers, or the ocean. A newly dead body usually sinks—at first. It will soon rise to the surface, however, and float there for the world to see. The reason submerged bodies bob back up has to do with the decomposition process. Bacteria instantly go to work inside a dead body, eating tissue and reproducing rapidly. These bacteria are anaerobic, meaning they do not require oxygen and other gases. Thus, they survive just as well underwater as anywhere. They do, however, create gases of their own as a byproduct of their feast on the body's tissues. As these gases build up under the skin, the dead body becomes a gas-filled buoy, gruesomely announcing its final resting place.

The Biology of Decomposition

Soon after death, a body begins to look much different than it appeared in life. The blood pools during livor mortis, leaving some parts of the body pale and bloodless and other parts purple or red with collected blood. The body's tissues lose their shape as individual cells die and burst apart, and these tissues come under attack by bacteria, the one-celled organisms that always live in and on the body but whose population are kept in check by the living body's immune system. Biologists examine the amount of bacterial growth that has taken place within a body to determine how long it has been since the person died.

White blood cells of the immune system patrol the body throughout its life, killing bacteria before they take over, multiply, and consume the body's cells and tissues. From the moment of death, however, the body's white blood cells are no longer on patrol, and the bacteria living inside the body, particularly in the intestines and the bowel, suddenly have

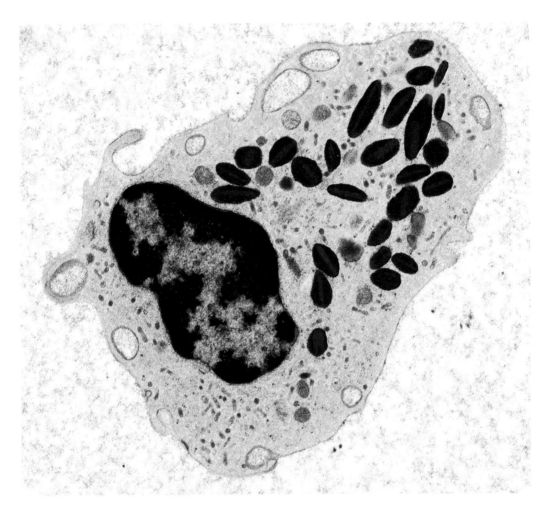

A magnified white blood cell, which combats bacteria within a living body, is colorized to show the detail of its structure. Upon death, white blood cell production stops, allowing bacteria to thrive and decomposition to begin.

freedom to feed on body tissues. Bacteria reproduce by splitting in half, so when they have a good food supply and no natural enemies to stop them, their population swells at an incredible pace. In only a few hours, a dead body's intestines and bowel teem with rapidly reproducing bacteria that eventually spread throughout the corpse. "Ground zero" for this process, the place where bacterial decomposition begins, is the cecum, a small pouch at the head of the large intestine that once held the bacteria the living body relied on to complete its digestion of food. "Typically," says science writer Jessica Snyder Sachs in her book *Corpse: Nature, Forensics, and the Struggle to Pinpoint Time of Death*, the bacteria's "booming population breaks through the intestinal wall two to three days [after death]."[18]

Microbiologists, scientists who study one-celled organisms such as bacteria, are able to track how fast bacteria grow in a dead body during the hours, days, and even weeks after death. They consider the temperature of the body and its surrounding environment to determine approximately how long a body must have been dead in order for bacterial growth to reach its current level. This process of bacteria's reproduction and spread throughout the body is called putrefaction.

"When we talk about decomposition, we usually mean putrefaction,"[19] say Vincent J. DiMaio and Dominick DiMaio in their book *Forensic Pathology*. The normal putrefaction process occurs in fairly predictable stages. Unless the temperature of the surrounding environment is extremely cold (which slows the growth of bacteria), evidence of putrefaction usually becomes obvious within a day or two after death. "The first outward sign appears as a subtle flush of green over the right lower abdomen, usually some twenty-four to forty-eight hours after death,"[20] says Sachs. The greenish color is caused by bacteria that grow and spread throughout the abdominal cavity; they devour the tissue there and give off a byproduct of gas as they feed. If the body is not discovered soon and refrigerated to stop further decomposition, the bacteria spread to other areas of the body. "They drift into the now passive circulation system," Sachs says, "following its stagnant streams up the chest, down the limbs, and across the face."[21] The head, neck, and shoulders take on a greenish hue, and the face swells as bacteria eat and release gases.

Within about three days, the entire body fills with gas, and the skin bloats with the pressure. As bacteria cause the body to swell, they give off sulfur-rich waste products and foul-smelling gases that bubble to the surface of the skin. By the time the body is discovered, a microbiologist may be able to tell, from the degree of decomposition, the approximate number of days that have passed since death, giving police a starting point to their investigation of a crime.

Steps in a Process: Rearing Insects to Determine Time of Death

When insects colonize a dead body, they go through stages of development, from eggs to larvae to adult insects. These stages take specific amounts of time, based on the insect species and the environmental conditions of the crime scene. Forensic entomologists often rear crime-scene insects in a laboratory to confirm the species and the length of time it takes the insects to mature, which in turn helps them determine time of death. This is how insects are reared:

1 Eggs and larvae are collected from the body at the crime scene.

2 Some of the eggs and larvae are put into preservatives to halt their development at the precise stage at which they were found.

3 Some of the eggs and larvae are transported immediately to an entomology lab to be reared into adult insects.

4 The entomologist separates the eggs from the larvae (some larvae and adult insects are cannibals and could eat important evidence).

5 Eggs and larvae are placed in aquariums or similar containers, with the same temperature and humidity that existed at the crime scene.

6 Raw meat, usually ground pork or beef, is placed in the aquariums as a food source.

7 The insects are carefully monitored as eggs hatch and larvae grow into adults.

8 The insect species is confirmed in adulthood, and the length of time for each developmental stage is documented.

The smell of putrefaction is important to time-of-death determinations for another reason: it attracts the attention of creatures that, like bacteria, thrive and reproduce on the flesh of the dead. These creatures are flies, and they colonize dead bodies, laying eggs so that their larvae, once they hatch, can feed on the body's decaying flesh. Because they have life cycles than can be measured precisely, flies are perhaps the most useful tool of all for helping investigators establish a time of death.

Forensic Flies

Of all the decomposition stages forensic scientists use to determine time of death, the presence of insects on the corpse is often the most accurate. Whereas the discoloration of livor mortis depends in part on the size of the victim, and the rate of bodily stiffening of rigor mortis may be affected by how active the person was at the moment of death, flies pay no attention to the size of a body or how suddenly it died. They merely notice dead flesh as a new place to lay eggs. And although the population of bacteria within a body takes time to reach a destructive level of decomposition, flies can detect a dead body—and move in on it—right away.

"Certain flies find the smell of death irresistible," says Sachs. "Within minutes, sometimes seconds, they materialize as if from thin air."[22] The flies' goal is to lay eggs on the soft, tender flesh that will provide the favorite food of their newly hatched young. "Just as in life," say DiMaio and DiMaio, "after death the tissues of humans are still attractive to insects."[23]

The reason flies are so useful for establishing time of death in a murder investigation is that each species of fly has a very predictable life span. "Insects follow a set pattern of development in or on the body,"[24] say DiMaio and DiMaio. When a fly lays eggs on a body, the eggs take a certain amount of time to hatch into maggots, the pale, worm-like larvae that feed on dead flesh. The maggots then go through a period of metamorphosis, during which they become adult flies. Depending on the species of fly, each of these stages takes a specific, measurable amount of time. "Identification of the type of insects present and their stage of development, in conjunction with knowledge of the rate of their development, can be used to determine approximately how long a body has been dead,"[25] DiMaio and DiMaio explain.

A forensic entomologist uses a microscope to identify the species of a fly found on the body of a murder victim.

Entomologists, scientists who specialize in the study of insects, can examine a fly egg or a maggot collected from a body, determine its species, and tell investigators how long that species takes to reach that stage of development. From this information, investigators make a good guess as to when the person died. Entomologists' professional opinion in making time-of-death determinations is important not just because they have the knowledge to identify which insect species are present on a body but also because they know

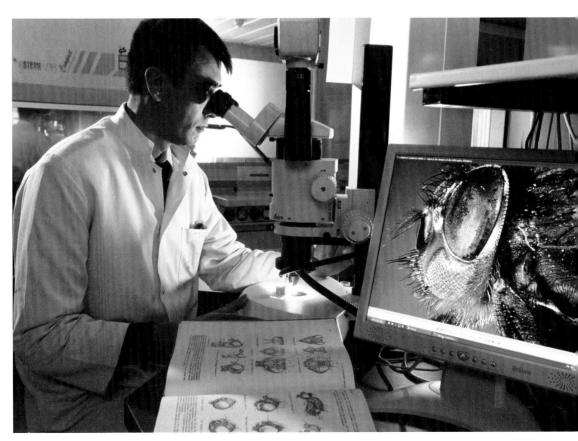

details about insect species that may be important to the investigation, such as the time of year a particular species is most active or the environmental conditions, such as temperature, that may affect a species' ability to reproduce.

"The time frame developed by the entomologist represents the minimum time the body has been dead,"[26] say Jay Dix and Michael A. Graham in their book *Time of Death, Decomposition and Identification: An Atlas.* A body may have been dead for a while before flies colonize it, they explain, and flies also are more likely to colonize a body during some seasons than others: "The entomologist is also able to determine what insects are active at particular times of the year and how long it typically takes for particular insects to invade the body."[27]

Establishing time of death based on insect activity requires close consideration not just of the insect species found on the body and its stage of development but of the conditions in which the body was found. "Varying factors, such as the rate of decomposition, burial, immersion in water, mummification, and geography, determine how soon and how many types and waves of insects will attack the body,"[28] say DiMaio and DiMaio. "Obviously, temperature and humidity are tied into seasons of the year, which also controls what insects are available."[29]

Even though an entomologist has many factors to consider when analyzing insects collected from a body, the importance of this evidence is clear. If a dead body contains fly larvae, it is proof that the body has been dead at least as long as it would take that particular species' maggots to reach their current stage of development. "Because the behavior and the life cycle of each insect species are so well documented," says Evans, "they can provide a reasonably accurate estimate of the time that has elapsed since death … accurate to the nearest day or week."[30]

By the Numbers

62

Number of professional forensic entomologists in the world.

Bugs and Bodies: A Longstanding Relationship

The presence of insects on a body has been used in murder investigations for centuries. One early case of forensic entomology occurred in a French boardinghouse in 1850 when a workman, while fixing a broken mantel, accidentally broke through the wall to the fireplace chimney and discovered the mummified body of a human infant. The young couple renting the room immediately became murder suspects, but the medical examiner in the case realized multiple sets of tenants had lived in the room during the previous three years. Only if he could establish a time of death could he prove which tenants had left the body in the chimney.

The medical examiner in the case, Dr. Marcel Bergeret, collected the cocoons left behind on the infant's body by the larvae that had already gone through metamorphosis into adult insects, and he deduced that the pupae came from a species of moth that only lays eggs on dried flesh that has been dead for

Bait for Beetles

Flies may be the first insects to detect a dead body, but they are rarely alone in colonizing it. Other flesh-eating insects are known to feast on cadavers—among them are carnivorous beetles. Maggots, the larvae that grow into flies at maturity, prefer flesh that is still moist, so they are abundant on a body in the early stages of decomposition. Some species of beetles, however, prefer flesh that is dry, and these wait patiently for the maggots to have their fill before they move in on the corpse. Still other beetles—such as the American carrion beetle—feed on maggots, and therefore, they coexist with fly larvae on a corpse. Entomologists can use any insect that remains on the body to help determine how long the person has been dead.

The carrion beetle is one of many insects that, when found on a body, can indicate to an entomologist how long a person has been dead.

some time. Based on this and his knowledge of the moth's life cycle, Bergeret decided the infant's body must have been in the chimney since 1849—the year before the current tenants moved into the room. The time of death, therefore, showed the current tenants to be innocent.

This case paved the way for the now common use of insect evidence to determine how long a body has been dead—an important fact for police to know as they investigate suspects in a murder case. "To this day," says Sachs, "Bergeret's clear

39

commentary on the successive [insect] colonization of a corpse stands out as a simple, yet sterling example of the tricky art of determining time of death."[31]

Decomposition Deadlines

Forensic scientists have limited time to perform their analyses on a dead body. Rigor mortis lasts only until bacteria start to consume the body, and bacteria, devouring tissue from the inside out, soon have to compete with insect larvae that eat the flesh from the outside in. Under most environmental conditions, the process of decomposition lasts only long enough for the body's moist tissue and organs to be consumed by bacteria and insects. At this point, bodies are mostly reduced to bone. If the body is not discovered until the flesh is gone, it may be difficult or impossible to establish time of death. Still, biology can contribute much to the investigation, because bones themselves can be important clues, often helping to establish the victim's identification.

CHAPTER 3

Reading the Bones

Depending on the environment in which a dead body is left, decomposition of soft tissues can happen in a period as short as a few days or weeks. Bacteria grow best in warm, moist places, and if the body is exposed to the environment in the summer, insects and their flesh-eating larvae are numerous. If this is the case, forensic investigators are left to investigate a body whose remaining skin and flesh is too sparse to tell them anything useful for the investigation.

Fortunately, the hard parts of a body—its bones and teeth— long outlast the soft tissues. Once a corpse has been cleaned down to its bones, bacteria die and insects move on. In his book *Cold Case Homicides*, Richard H. Walton says that "if the case is cold because the remains are found long after death, bones and teeth may be the only sources of data for identification."[32] When an unexpected skeleton is discovered, investigators often call a forensic anthropologist to the scene, an expert in the study and identification of human skeletal remains.

Recovering Bones

There is a scientific method to removing or collecting a skeleton from its final resting place, and an anthropologist's skilled direction ensures that valuable evidence, such as a skeleton's smallest bones, does not get lost or overlooked as the body is exhumed, or removed, from its resting place. "Meticulous excavation combined with a trained anthropological eye can yield clues missed by others,"[33] says anthropologist Stanley Rhine. "The forensic anthropologist cannot analyze skeletal material that he or she does not have. Recovery is thus the essential first link in skeletal analysis."[34]

Unearthing a skeleton involves the same careful steps as the excavation of an archaeological dig. The tools used are trowels

Forensic experts undertake the painstaking process of excavating skeletons found at a construction site, with the goal of collecting and preserving the remains as completely as possible.

and brushes, wooden picks for gently teasing out the edges of the buried bones, buckets to haul away excavated soil, and a screen for sifting the dirt to look for small pieces of bone or evidence. The body is uncovered one thin layer of dirt at a time. "Digging a small deep hole may be good exercise," says Rhine, "but it is poor recovery technique."[35]

The goals of excavation are to recover the remains as completely as possible and to make a record, in diagrams and pictures, of how the body was positioned in its grave. "A grave is a crime scene," says Walton. "It is a potential source of evidence, and must be handled with care by trained personnel."[36] All evidence collected from the burial site is carefully labeled, packaged, and transported to a crime lab for further study. The bones are pieced together and laid out in their precise skeletal formation, and the anthropologist then makes important determinations from the bones—beginning with whether they are, indeed, human.

Steps in a Process: Excavating a Body

When a human grave is discovered, it is important to uncover the body carefully, one layer of dirt at a time, to make sure that important fragments of evidence such as plant material or shards of bone are collected. Here are the steps for properly excavating a body:

1 The ground over the grave is cleared of vegetation.

2 The perimeter, or outside edge, of the grave site are marked with stakes to create an outline of the grave.

3 A trench is dug alongside the grave so excavators can remove the body from the side instead of digging down from the top; this minimizes damage to the remains.

4 Soil is removed from the grave site in shallow layers, and each layer is sifted through a sieve to search for tiny bone fragments or pieces of evidence.

5 When the body is completely uncovered, it is photographed before the remains are lifted out as a whole.

6 The grave is excavated down to sterile soil, still sifting the dirt for remaining evidence.

7 An inventory is made of the contents of the grave before the pieces are packaged and labeled.

Man, Not Beast

The findings of the forensic anthropologist can lead to the precise identity of a missing person, but before they spend time analyzing skeletal remains to calculate such details as a person's gender and age, anthropologists first make sure that the bones originally came from a person. Humans are not the only species whose bones sometimes turn up outdoors, and the discovery of nonhuman bones has launched many unnecessary forensic investigations. "It is an expensive mistake if a police investigation is initiated on the misidentification of animal bone,"[37] say forensic bone analysts Louise Scheuer and Sue Black.

To find out whether a crime has taken place, the anthropologist needs to know whether the bones belonged to an animal or a human being. The problem is not always easy to sort out. Certainly, the skulls and teeth of most animals look very different from the skulls and teeth of humans. A dog's skull, for example, is long and has large, pointed canine teeth. A human skull is rounder, with room for a bigger brain and with flat, straight teeth. A human skull's eye sockets face forward, and the hole at the base, where the skull attaches to the spine, is positioned for walking upright (as opposed to most other animals, which walk on all fours and whose spines attach at a different point on their skulls). Few people mistake an animal skull for a human one, but the skull is not always found with other bones at the scene, or it may have been broken into pieces too small to recognize as human.

In the absence of a skull, it is easy to mistake the bones of an animal for the bones of a human. Rhine describes one such case in which a set of bones was discovered near Albuquerque, New Mexico. No skull was present, but just the same, investigators deduced that the bones were those of a twelve-year-old girl. "The sheriff informed the media, who ran with these 'facts' to blast the populace of Albuquerque with stories on television, on the radio, and in print,"[38] Rhine says. Several days later, the pathologist examining the bones discovered the ribcage had too many ribs to belong to a human. It was, in fact, the skeleton of a bear—a fact that an anthropologist would have realized far sooner, had one been called to collect and analyze the bones.

"Every animal's species has distinct characteristics for identification of its bones and teeth,"[39] says forensic scientist J. R. Gaur. Forensic anthropologists are skilled in this level of identification and can quickly separate nonhuman remains from human ones. Once they identify the latter, they look for additional clues the bones can provide as to the identity of the person.

Becoming a Forensic Anthropologist

Job Description:
When human remains are discovered, a forensic anthropologist assists with the recovery and excavation of all parts of the body and related evidence at the site. The anthropologist examines the remains to establish identifying characteristics such as gender, age, and race.

Education:
Forensic anthropologists have a doctorate degree in physical anthropology and may specialize in additional fields such as osteology, dentistry, or pathology.

Qualifications:
Experience and training in human anatomy and identification as well as fieldwork experience in the excavation of human remains are essential for forensic anthropologists. Certification by the American Board of Forensic Anthropology is optional and requires a doctorate degree and three years of full-time work experience.

Additional Information:
Full-time jobs for forensic anthropologists are mostly offered by the government, the military, or the police departments of large cities. Many forensic anthropologists work for museums or universities and do forensic consulting part-time.

Salary:
$45,000 to more than $70,000 per year

Clues from Bone

When an anthropologist determines that skeletal remains are human, the search begins for additional clues. Bones reveal many things to an anthropologist, and the more complete the skeleton, the more the bones reveal. In the best scenario, when an entire skeleton has been recovered from the burial site, anthropologists are usually 100 percent accurate in determining whether the bones belonged to a man or a woman. They can determine gender from the skull alone 90 percent of the time; if they have just the pelvis (hip bones), their accuracy at identifying the gender jumps to 95 percent. "Even incomplete or fragmentary remains can yield useful information to a person trained in their analysis,"[40] says Walton.

Additional details that a skeleton provides include the person's approximate age and height at the time of death, and sometimes the person's probable race or ethnicity as well.

Investigators study a set of excavated skeletal remains to determine identity and cause of death. The damage to the skull indicates that the victim met a violent death.

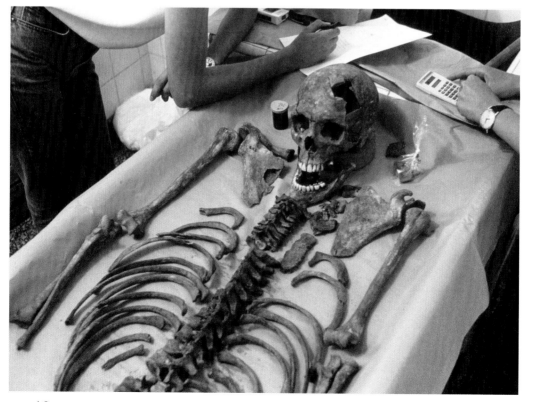

Anthropologists also look for evidence of injuries or medical conditions of the bone. All of these clues are valuable to the death investigation because they help police narrow down the list of known missing persons to whom the bones might belong. Once a forensic anthropologist has confirmed that bones are human, say Scheuer and Black, he or she "must attempt to personalize the information available so that individual identity is achieved."[41]

The length of the femur (thigh bone), the largest bone in the human body, correlates to a person's overall height.

Guessing Height from Bones

Human bones contain a wealth of information, but it takes years of training to properly examine them. Osteology, the scientific study of bones, is a specialty of biology that requires specific training in growth, formation, injury, and disease of bone tissue. Forensic anthropologists depend on their knowledge of human osteology to help them determine a body's gender, height, age, and other factors that might help police identify a murder victim. As Scheuer and Black note, the science of forensic osteology "is not something that can be learned from a textbook in a single year. It is a subject that relies heavily on practical experience that must be gained over time."[42]

Some important osteological determinations, however, are fairly straightforward and measurable. Estimating an individual's height, or stature, is one of these. Because the length of every long bone—for example, the femur, the bone of the thigh—has a direct relationship to the overall height of the individual, height can usually be calculated to within a couple of inches, or about five centimeters. "It is difficult to make a major mistake in the calculation of stature,"[43] says Rhine.

Determining a person's race and gender also is useful when estimating height, because the bones of men and women and of people who belong to different ethnic groups tend to grow to slightly different lengths. The average man, for instance, is typically taller and has longer bones than the average woman, and an average Caucasian person is slightly taller than the average person of Asian descent. To get the best estimate of an unknown victim's height, therefore, forensic anthropologists also analyze bones for clues about gender and ethnicity.

Race and Gender Indicators

The pelvic bones of the hip area give valuable clues about gender. A woman's hips are uniquely shaped for bearing and giving birth to children, and they have enough differences from a man's that anthropologists can guess gender very accurately from pelvic bones. If a woman has given birth in her lifetime, there may be additional changes to her pelvis, making the correct identification of her gender even more likely.

The skull, too, helps anthropologists determine gender, and it can offer other information as well. Men usually have heavier cheekbones and a broader, thicker jaw than women, for example, while women tend to have larger, rounder eyes that sit slightly higher in the face. The size and slope of the eyes and the width of the nose are traits that differ among many of

Differences in shape between the male pelvis, left, and the female pelvis, right, aid investigators in determining gender as part of identifying skeletal remains.

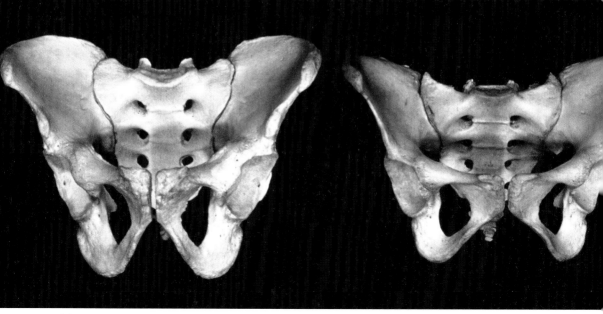

the world's ethnic groups, and these differences in living faces are also reflected in the features of skulls.

While people of a common ethnic origin do tend to have distinctive features, most people in the United States today, however, are a mix of multiple ethnicities, which can make it difficult to determine the exact race to which a skeleton belongs. According to Scheuer and Black, "the determination of race or ethnic origin is the most difficult and unreliable attribute that the forensic osteologist must attempt to establish."[44]

> ## By the Numbers
>
> # 80%
>
> **Accuracy rate for identifying gender from a skeleton's arm and leg bones alone.**

Telling Age from Bones

Another important clue that human bones reveal to forensic anthropologists is how old the person was at the time of his or her death. Bones change throughout a person's life. They grow a great deal between birth and maturity, and then they become increasingly brittle throughout adulthood. Because the bones of all humans, regardless of ethnicity or gender, grow and change, it is often possible for anthropologists to determine from skeletal remains the approximate age a person was at the time of death.

Bones belonging to a child are smaller, thinner, and shorter than bones from an adult, and they are recognizable as juvenile bones because of evidence that they are still growing. To make room for growth, tough, flexible tissue, called cartilage, caps the long arm and leg bones of children and adolescents. Only when these bones reach maturity do these caps, or epiphyses, turn into solid bone. Thus, an anthropologist can identify the bones of a child or teenager by the amount of cartilage that caps the long bones of the arms and legs. Many bones also fuse to other bones once human growth is complete. "A human comes into this world with 450 separate pieces, which later fuse, either wholly or partially, to create the 206-bone inventory

Murder at Harvard

In November 1849 Dr. George Parkman visited Harvard University to collect some money that was owed to him. He was never seen alive again. Dr. George Webster was the university professor Parkman went to see, and although he insisted he had paid Parkman back in full, the case became suspicious when a janitor at the college found human hip and leg bones at the bottom of Webster's laboratory privy (the 1800s version of a toilet). Other body parts, including a man's torso, were later found in Webster's laboratory, and Webster was arrested for Parkman's murder. The court case was filled with medical testimony on whether a body missing its head could be identified by bones alone. Groundbreaking evidence came from Parkman's dentist, who produced a mold

Tarps cover two bodies placed for study in an outdoor research site known as the Body Farm, which is utilized by the University of Tennessee's Forensic Anthropology Center in order to study various aspects of human decomposition.

he had once made of Parkman's jaw to craft false teeth. A few teeth recovered from the crime scene fit precisely into this mold. In the end, Webster was convicted and hanged for first-degree murder. It was the first death sentence given in the United States for a murder in which there was no complete corpse, just some of its bones.

of an adult,"[45] says Sachs. When anthropologists see a juvenile skeleton in which some of the bones have matured but others have not, they can determine approximately how old the skeleton's owner must have been at the time he or she died.

Even in adult skeletons, it is often possible to identify the approximate age of the victim. Lifelong use of the body takes its toll on bones and joints. "The wear and tear of aging," says Sachs, "leaves joints pitted and craggy."[46] Rhine says bones also take on certain physical features from a lifetime of particular postures and repetitive movements. "Each skeleton is adjusted to the specific needs set by the posture and activity of its owner and operator,"[47] he says. Such patterns of wear can be clues about the age of the person to whom the bones belong.

Tracking Down Missing Persons

Whenever a person goes missing, the absence is usually reported to the police. The individual's personal information is then recorded in a database. Police who are investigating the discovery of unknown human remains eventually compare these remains to a file of known missing persons, hoping to exclude all records but one, and thus, reach a positive identification for the victim.

Because missing-persons files contain many records, forensic anthropologists can be a tremendous help to narrowing down the search. For each missing person in the database, there is a record of details such as gender, race, height, weight, date of birth, and known medical conditions. If the forensic anthropologist can correctly identify a victim's gender, this alone cuts in half the number of records. When details such as age, height, and race are also known, the list of possible matches becomes shorter still. These details, say Scheuer and Black, "allow a preliminary picture to be built regarding the possible identity of the deceased and permit targeting of specific aspects of a missing persons register."[48]

Once the forensic anthropologist has studied the available bones and arrived at scientific estimates of the person's gender, height, race, and age, police can use the information to look through missing-persons files more efficiently, focusing only on records of people who have characteristics similar to the anthropologist's profile. When they are down to a few possible matches, they begin the much more involved and technical process of determining whether the victim's characteristics exactly match those of a missing person.

Forensic anthropologists make educated guesses based on human remains. Any definite match between bones from a crime scene and the identity of missing person, however, must be based on evidence that can be proven. Therefore, police may track down extra information from the medical records of each missing person who is a possible match for the bones. Of particular interest for identification purposes are dental records.

A Toothy Subject

People are born with a standard set of twenty baby teeth that begin to emerge in the first few months of life. These baby teeth fall out during childhood and are replaced by thirty-two permanent teeth. The way adult teeth grow in and the dental treatments they receive through life are unique to each individual. Forensic odontologists are the experts who use these unique characteristics of teeth to help match missing persons to unidentified corpses by means of dental features.

In the United States, most people make regular visits to a dentist. X-rays are a routine part of these dental checkups, because they give the dentist a record of how teeth are growing through childhood and adulthood. Regular x-rays of the teeth and jaws provide a useful way for dentists to track their patients' unique dental problems, such as cavities or shifting teeth, and treatments over the years. These x-rays are kept on file so the dentist can assess how the teeth have grown and changed, and they are part of a person's permanent dental records, meaning they can be transferred to new dentists if the patient moves. Dental records also can be requested by police departments if a missing patient is believed to be a match for an unidentified corpse. The missing person's closest living relative often provides written consent for the dentist to release these records. Police also can get a court order for dental records they need.

Dental records are one of the most useful tools for confirming the identity of an unnamed body. "Dental identification is an important method of postmortem identification," says forensic dentistry expert James H. Hardy. Sometimes it may be the only method that can be used to make or rule out an identification. "The dental structures and dental restorations (filings, etc.) may be the only parts of the body not destroyed,"[49] Hardy says.

Dental x-rays and other records are frequently used to identify skeletal remains, as the problems and procedures they show are unique to the individual.

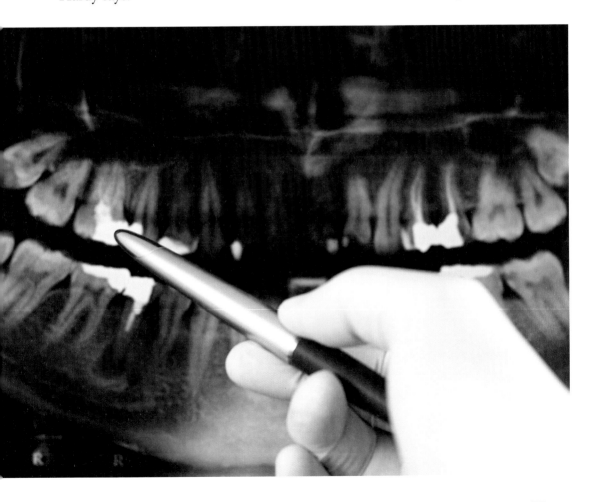

Dental records and x-rays are useful for victim identification because they provide evidence of many unique processes and problems that occurred in the mouth of a missing person—problems that are either consistent with a murder victim's teeth or not. For instance, dentists keep records of cavities, which can be filled with any of several common materials, including silver, gold, and composite. Descriptions of each filling are written down by the patient's dentist, and fillings also will appear in a missing person's dental x-rays. If the jaw of a corpse has no dental filling in tooth number twenty-nine, but the dental records of a missing person reveal a gold filling in tooth twenty-nine, the teeth cannot be from the same person. The corpse's tooth, which is lacking the filling, cannot belong to a missing person who received a filling in that tooth.

Absent teeth can be another useful tool for comparing dental records of missing persons to a jaw found at a crime scene. If a missing person had all of her wisdom teeth extracted, for example, but the skull at the crime scene shows a jaw with all of its wisdom teeth present, the forensic odontologist will conclude the two teeth patterns cannot come from the same person. Wisdom teeth, once removed, do not grow back in; the victim must be someone whose wisdom teeth were never pulled.

It is easier to rule out a possible dental match between an unidentified body and a missing person than to confirm that two sets of teeth are a definite match. If a missing person's dental x-rays show that all the wisdom teeth are gone, and if a corpse also is missing all of its wisdom teeth, the forensic odontologist still cannot conclude that the jaws are from the same person. It is common for wisdom teeth to be removed, so any number of potential missing-person matches could be missing their wisdom teeth. It also is common for teeth to fall out of a skeleton's jaw as a corpse decomposes or gets moved or damaged at its burial site. This can lead investigators to think that the wisdom teeth were missing at the time of death when they actually fell out afterward.

Making a positive identification of victims using their dental records is rarely easy. Dental records collected for patients in the missing-persons database are not always complete or recent enough to be helpful. Even when good dental records exist, different dentists keep different kinds of records. Some records are more complete and descriptive than others. "It has been stated that more than 150 types of records are currently in regular use in the U.S. alone,"[50] says Hardy. In addition, he says, there are different charting systems to record the position of patients' teeth in the mouth, and "there are also different methods used in different countries to identify different surfaces of the teeth."[51] These differences in recordkeeping make it hard to compare one set of tooth records to another, or to a corpse whose identity is in question.

Even when all the teeth of an unidentified body have been kept together and are intact in the jaw after death, matching them to the dental records of a missing person can be a challenge. At some crime scenes, however, full sets of teeth are never found. In such cases, forensic odontologists face even greater difficulty. They must rely on their ability to identify individual teeth and where these teeth belong in the human mouth. They may even be asked to try to make an identification based on just one remaining tooth. Nonetheless, a dental identification may be possible. Perhaps the remaining tooth is a molar with an unusual feature, such as a crack or a filling that exactly matches the same molar in a missing person's dental records. Thus, even when a missing person's dental records are incomplete or when most of a corpse's teeth have fallen out and been scattered, forensic odontology could lead investigators to the victim's identity. Dental records often rule out some possible matches completely, and they can suggest that the victim's remaining teeth are a strong match to those of a missing person. "When all is said and done," says Hardy, human dentition "may have the last word."[52]

Solid Identification

Forensic odontologists have one other, secret weapon in the depths of each tooth. Teeth hold a unique, carefully protected key to the indisputable identity of a corpse. Deep inside each tooth, beneath the hard layers of enamel, there is a root and a tiny, well protected pocket of soft material called pulp. The pulp of every tooth holds a person's DNA. Sheltered by the strong armor of the tooth surface, this tooth DNA may be the one thing that outlasts the rest of the body at a crime scene, often surviving mutilation and decomposition of the corpse, even by fire. The task of extracting DNA from a tooth and using it to positively identify a victim falls to experts in the analysis of tissues and body fluids found at crime scenes.

Body Fluids Left Behind

Blood has always been an important clue in cases of violent crime. The average-sized person has about 10 pints (4.73l) of blood in his or her arteries and veins, and, for this blood to leak out, an injury must occur. The presence of blood alone is valuable evidence that a violent crime has taken place, even if the injured body is no longer at the scene. But forensic scientists who specialize in the collection and analysis of blood use it to identify the individual it came from, making blood an extremely valuable form of evidence in a criminal case.

Some homicide victims bleed to death, and their blood covers the ground, floor, or other surfaces of the crime scene. At other scenes, blood may be found when the body is not. Even when investigators do not find a body, they can sometimes determine that a murder took place. A person who loses 4 pints (2l) or more of blood at one time will not survive. If police find at least this much of the same person's blood at the crime scene, they conclude that the victim bled to death. They know they are investigating a murder, even if the body that produced the blood is no longer at the scene.

Blood is such an important clue in criminal cases that it has launched a distinct branch of forensic biology—serology. Serology is the collection, identification, and analysis of blood and other body fluids from victims, suspects, and crime scenes. These fluids can establish a solid link between a suspect, a victim, and the scene of a crime. To use blood evidence convincingly in court, however, investigators must prove three things: that the fluid at the crime scene is, in fact, blood; that it came from a human being; and which human being, specifically, it came from.

DUIs: Proof in the Bottle
Leads to Proof in the Blood

One of the most common crimes in the United States is driving while under the influence of alcohol or drugs. With every beer or cocktail a person consumes, alcohol seeps into the bloodstream. People who drink and drive carry the proof of their crime in their own veins. Blood alcohol content is the ratio of alcohol to blood in a person's body, and serologists can quickly determine this ratio with a simple blood test. If there is just one gram of alcohol for every five hundred grams of blood in the body, the blood alcohol content is 0.20—more than twice the legal limit a driver is allowed to have (it is against the law in any state in the United States to drive with a blood alcohol content of more than 0.08, and in some states, the limit is even lower). Detecting drunk drivers and proving their guilt is one of the quickest and most effective uses of forensic serology.

Highway patrol officers observe a driver during a field sobriety test. Such tests may provide officers with preliminary information about whether a driver is impaired, but a test that measures the presence of alcohol in the blood provides foolproof evidence in drunk driving arrests.

Trail of Evidence

Whenever there is blood at the scene of a crime, it could be important proof that a victim or a suspect was at that particular place. In order for serologists to perform the series of tests on the blood that determine whether it is human, and if so, who it came from, the blood must first be identified and collected. This is not always a straightforward process. While some bodies are found lying in a pool of blood, at other crime scenes, blood is not so easy to find. Sometimes, a mere speck, drop, or smear suggests blood could be present. But blood, when it dries, turns dark brown and can be confused with other things, such as stains used to finish wood. Investigators may collect samples of any substance they find at the scene, but if the substance is not blood, it is not useful to a serologist. "When a darkish substance is found at a crime scene, it must first be determined to be blood,"[53] says forensic scientist Katherine Ramsland, Ph.D., so that expensive and time-consuming identification tests are not mistakenly performed on samples of other substances.

A forensic technician holds a sample of dried blood found at a crime scene. Even a small amount of blood can provide a great deal of information about a crime.

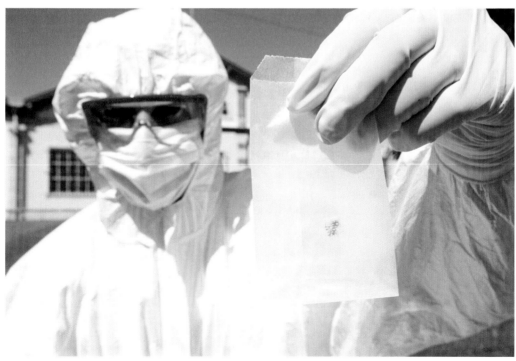

Any trace of blood, however small, could be important evidence. A tiny drop of a murder victim's blood in the car or apartment of a man who claims he never met her is powerful evidence in court. Therefore, investigators routinely examine crime scenes for traces of blood evidence. They often begin by moving a powerful light across every surface of the scene in search of suspicious droplets or specks.

If a suspicious drop or stain is found, a crime scene technician needs a quick way to determine whether or not the specimen should be collected for further analysis. "For practical reasons," say Joe Nickell and John F. Fischer in their book *Crime Science*, "it is customary to first identify a suspect substance as blood before proceeding to more complex tests."[54] One method for doing this is the Kastle-Meyer color test. A swab of the substance suspected to be blood is smeared on a slip of filter paper that contains a chemical called phenolphthalein, which turns bright pink when exposed to even a tiny amount of blood. This test is a quick and easy way to determine whether visible stains at the scene of a crime are blood that should be collected as evidence in the case.

There may be more blood at a scene that escapes the human eye, even in bright light. Blood droplets are sometimes tiny and can be hidden under furniture or masked by colorful fabric such as a patterned bedspread. Some murderers also clean up after their crimes, wiping down surfaces and shampooing carpets so well that bloodstains seem to vanish. In older cases that have remained unsolved for a period of time, finding new blood evidence is even more difficult. There is a chemical, however, that investigators use to find even latent, or hidden, blood stains—tiny drops of blood on a wall or a wood floor that investigators overlooked, for instance, or blood stains in fabric, on walls, or on carpets that have been mopped up until they are no longer visible to the naked eye. The chemical is called luminol, and if human blood is or ever has been present at a crime scene, luminol will bring it to light.

First, a solution is created by dissolving crystals of luminol—a powdery chemical compound of nitrogen, hydrogen, oxygen, and carbon—in liquid hydrogen peroxide. When the luminol solution comes into contact with any amount of iron, a chemical reaction takes place, and the luminol gives off a faint blue light in a chemical process called chemiluminescence. All blood has iron in the form of hemoglobin—the proteins in red blood cells that use iron to bind to oxygen molecules and carry them to body tissues. Iron is present in any amount of blood, large or small, fresh or dried, and it reacts with luminol to glow blue in a dark room.

"Ironically, the [luminol] test is most effective on older stains," say Nickell and Fischer. "Even the smear marks caused by wiping or mopping, in attempts to remove bloodstains, can often be 'visualized' by use of this test."[55] Blood evidence, invisible to the naked eye, has been identified by luminol even after blood-stained surfaces have been scrubbed repeatedly with powerful cleaning agents. Luminol revealed the presence of century-old blood in the former home of Lizzie Borden, a young woman who went on trial in 1893 when she was accused of murdering her father and stepmother with a hatchet. The Borden home in Fall River, Massachusetts, is now a bed-and-breakfast inn, but investigators who tested it with luminol found that blood stains in crevices of the floorboards still glowed blue more than a hundred years after the Borden murders.

Identifying the presence of blood at a suspected crime scene is only the first step in using it as evidence. Blood is most useful in criminal cases when it can be traced back to one specific individual, such as a victim or a suspect of a murder, but determining who blood belongs to involves expensive and time-consuming analyses. Before launching such an intensive study of blood, investigators first perform tests to determine whether the blood they have found is human.

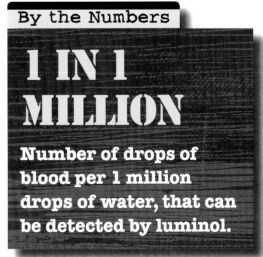

By the Numbers

1 IN 1 MILLION

Number of drops of blood per 1 million drops of water, that can be detected by luminol.

Human versus Animal Blood

On May 1, 2007, a thirty-seven-year-old woman was reported missing in Plainfield, Illinois. Blood was found in the bed of her husband's truck, but he claimed that the blood was not suspicious in the least—he recently had used the truck for hunting, he said, so the blood was from deer and rabbits. Similar excuses have been used by suspects in murder cases for hundreds of years.

Investigators need a way to test the blood found on a suspect's belongings to determine if it came from a human rather than an animal. The presence of human blood, in a place where a suspect insisted only animal blood should be, suggests that the suspect may be lying. If, on the other hand, the blood did come from an animal after all, an innocent person may be spared the horror of being investigated for a murder. Fortunately, investigators have a quick way to tell whether a suspect is lying about the origin of blood.

At the turn of the twentieth century, a Viennese doctor named Paul Uhlenhuth discovered that when serum, the liquid portion of blood, was taken from a rabbit and combined with a sample of human blood, the mixture instantly turned cloudy. Even more importantly, say Colin Wilson and Damon Wilson in their book *Written in Blood*, Uhlenhuth found that rabbit serum "would react just as well to a bloodstain dissolved in salt water."[56] Uhlenhuth had discovered the precipitin test—a test still used today to look for the telltale cloudiness, or solid precipitant, that results when any trace of human blood is added to a test tube of rabbit serum.

This new method of blood testing led to the conviction of German serial killer Ludwig Tessnow in 1901. Tessnow, a carpenter, claimed that the dark spots someone noticed on his clothes came from wood stain. A farmer insisted they were stains from sheep that Tessnow had killed, and investigators suspected something more sinister still—that the stains actually came from the blood of several children who had been brutally murdered. Uhlenhuth tested the stains from Tessnow's overalls and found that seventeen of them were

Biologist Paul Uhlenhuth discovered the precipitin test, which enables the identification of human blood.

Becoming a Forensic Serologist

Job Description:
The forensic serologist finds and collects traces of body fluids on objects from crime scenes and performs genetic tests on this evidence. The serologist prepares reports of scientific findings and may be expected to testify in court.

Education:
Forensic serologists hold a bachelor's or master's degree in forensic or biological science, with courses in biochemistry, genetics, DNA analysis, and molecular biology.

Qualifications:
To be considered for a job as a forensic serologist, at least one year of work or internship experience in forensic DNA analysis is required.

Additional Information:
Forensic serologists must be familiar with chemical and laboratory equipment and the computer software used to create reports. They sometimes respond to crime scenes to collect evidence and may also appear in court to testify about their findings.

Salary:
$40,000 to $55,000 per year

indeed human blood. Uhlenhuth's method led to Tessnow's execution for murder in 1904, and it has been used in countless cases since.

"The precipitin test is extremely sensitive, requiring only minute blood samples," says Colin Evans in *The Casebook of Forensic Detection*. "Positive results have been obtained on human blood that has been dried for as long as fifteen years."[57] It is no longer easy for people to explain suspicious blood stains by blaming them on animals. Some killers, however, make a false claim that the blood is their own and that it came from a nosebleed or a personal injury. To disprove such statements, serologists look for unique proteins found in different people's blood.

Blood Types

In the late 1800s, at about the same time that Uhlenhuth discovered the precipitin test, a doctor named Leonard Landais discovered another property of blood. He was making early attempts at life-saving transfusions of blood from animals to humans, but when animal blood was injected into human veins, the results were disastrous. Red blood cells from the animal species reacted with red blood cells of people and "clumped together like lumps in porridge,"[58] say Wilson and Wilson. Blood from one human sometimes had the same result when added to the blood of another human. "There could be only one

A laboratory technician conducts a test to determine the type of a sample of blood, based on the proteins present on the blood cells.

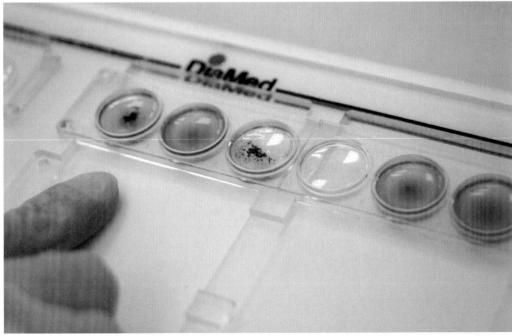

answer," Wilson and Wilson explain. "There must be several types of human blood."[59]

Landais had made an important discovery. Human beings have different proteins on the surfaces of their red blood cells. One person's blood cells may have clumping proteins that cause red blood cells to stick to other red blood cells. Another person's cells may have repelling proteins, which prevent them from sticking to others. The types of proteins on the surfaces of red blood cells lead to different blood types in the human population. These blood types explain why blood from one person sometimes clumps when mixed with blood from another person: not all human blood is the same.

The four main human blood types are A, B, AB, and O. The differences are based on the proteins on the surfaces of a person's blood cells. Blood types are important for medical reasons—only people with compatible blood types can be blood donors during transfusions, for example. But blood types are also useful in helping crime investigators narrow down the list of people to whom blood at a crime scene could belong.

Once a blood type has been determined, investigators may be able to rule out some of the suspects. If the blood found on a murder suspect's jeans is type A, for instance, but the suspect's own blood type is O, the suspect cannot claim that the blood on his jeans came from a cut on his own finger. If the victim in the case also has a blood type of A, the blood on the suspect's jeans could be the victim's. On the other hand, if the victim has a blood type of AB, the blood on the suspect's jeans could *not* have come from that victim.

Blood typing is an important screening tool to help investigators narrow down possible suspects in a case or rule out suspects altogether. "The goal is to reach—or at least approach as closely as possible—the individuation of a sample of blood,"[60] say Nickell and Fischer. By individuation, they mean narrowing down the number of people to whom the blood could belong until there is just one individual left. "Preliminary blood tests are called 'presumptive' tests; that is, they are used for screening,"[61] Nickell and Fischer explain. When preliminary tests suggest there may be a positive link between a suspect, a victim, and/or a scene, this is the green light for serologists to begin the time-consuming and expensive process of confirming blood identity using DNA.

When Blood Gets Personal

Every cell of the human body has a nucleus that acts as the cell's control center, and every nucleus contains two strands of deoxyribonucleic acid, or DNA, twisted together into a complex molecule of genetic information. DNA acts as an instruction manual. It contains all the information that the cells of every tissue need to do their jobs in the body. "DNA provides a 'computer program' that determines our physical features and many other attributes,"[62] says DNA analyst John M. Butler, Ph.D.

All people's DNA holds the same instructions needed to make a body human, but every person's DNA also is different than that of every other human. The differences are very slight. Only a tiny percentage of human DNA differs from one person to the next. These differences, however, are what make each of us look a little different, and they are what forensic serologists use to prove that DNA collected from a crime scene could have come from one and only one person on earth.

DNA is exclusive evidence, meaning that it can be used to exclude every suspect in a murder case except one. Blood types are much easier to determine than DNA profiles but may only exclude some suspects. "An ABO blood group determination…can be performed in a few minutes," says Butler, "but it is not very informative. There are only four possible groups that are typed—A, B, AB, and O."[63] Nearly one-half of the U.S. population has the blood type O, for example, so it is probable that one-half of the suspects in a murder case will also have the blood type O. If the blood from the crime scene is type O as well, this means than on average, half of the suspects will not be ruled out by blood type alone. DNA, however, would quickly

A forensic technician collects a cigarette butt as a piece of evidence at a crime scene. DNA evidence can be lifted from items that come in contact with body fluid, such as saliva, thus establishing—or eliminating—a connection between a suspect and a crime.

tell the difference between the suspects and could link one, without any doubt, to the scene.

Blood, however, useful to a serologist, is not the only bodily fluid that contains DNA. Suspects and victims can leave DNA at the crime scene or on one another's bodies or clothing even if neither bleeds. DNA evidence can be pulled from traces of many body fluids, including semen, saliva, and urine, left behind during a crime either accidentally or deliberately. The most common fluid analyzed for DNA, in fact, is not blood but semen, which is present in some murders and in almost all instances of rape. When rape victims seek medical help, a rape kit helps doctors collect semen samples. This evidence will provide a DNA profile that can later be matched to a list of suspects in the case. If the DNA profile found at the crime scene matches the DNA profile of a suspect, this evidence can be used in court to prove his guilt. When profiles of two different DNA samples match, the chance that the samples did not come from the same person is a fraction of 1 percent.

DNA also is found in saliva, which may be present at a crime scene if the perpetrator bit the victim, for example, but also if he smoked a cigarette and left the butt behind, sipped a soda and tossed the can away, or spit out a piece of chewing gum. Urine, too, holds DNA evidence and is sometimes present at crime scenes. Some perpetrators urinate at the scenes of their crimes, but some victims also urinate in terror, and DNA from this urine can be an important clue in a case. Finding DNA from a victim's urine in a suspect's vehicle, for instance, can prove that the victim was in the suspect's car, even if no blood is found. "Scientific research has advanced analytic technology so that the DNA molecule can now be used as the standard for characterization of all biologic samples,"[64] say serologists Rosalind Bowman, Teri Labbe, and Kimberly

By the Numbers

81%

Percentage of DNA crime laboratories in the U.S. that say they are backlogged with cases.

Mullings. During the past two decades, improvements in the collection, analysis, and comparison of human DNA samples have changed the field of forensic science.

Reading the DNA

Finding, collecting, and processing this DNA is now one of the most common applications of forensic biology, but in its early days, DNA processing was a slow and expensive process that sometimes made investigations lag for weeks. Geneticists first realized there were specific sequences in each human's DNA in 1985, but computers were slow to make the necessary DNA comparisons. Modern computers have improved the speed of DNA analysis dramatically. "DNA testing that previously took 6 or 8 weeks can now be performed in a few hours,"[65] says Butler. Faster processing is also aided by better collection methods—crime scene technicians now gather samples of any substance, wet or dry, that might contain DNA evidence, using sterile, cotton-tipped swabs that are available just for this purpose.

Planted at the Scene

DNA from plants is as useful as human DNA in some criminal cases. When a murdered woman's body was found at an abandoned factory in Maricopa County, Arizona, in 1993, the main suspect told police he had never been to the place. Two seed pods in the bed of his truck said otherwise. They came from a blue Palo Verde tree, the same kind of tree growing along the factory's driveway. A plant geneticist compared DNA from the seed pods in the truck to that of the crime scene's tree. The DNA was a close match, but it was not similar to samples from twenty other blue Palo Verde trees in the surrounding area. The evidence strongly suggested that the pods in the suspect's truck were from the exact tree at the factory, casting doubt on his claim that he had never been to the factory before.

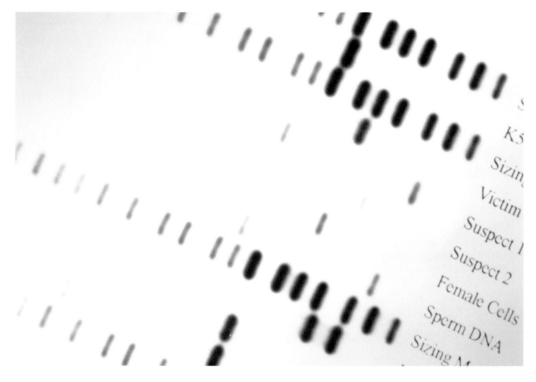

When these swabs are taken to a forensic serologist's laboratory, the serologist extracts a strand of DNA from each of them and puts it through a chemical process that quickly makes copies. The ability to copy DNA, creating a large sample from a tiny one, has a huge benefit in criminal cases—a tiny trace of blood, saliva, urine, or semen is all that needs to be collected to create a DNA profile. "Results can be reliably obtained in as little as a few hours from a very small drop of blood or a bloodstain,"[66] says Butler. Once a DNA profile has been created, it becomes a powerful tool investigators can use to search for the one person to whom it belongs.

An autoradiograph compares DNA profiles of suspects in a rape investigation with evidence collected from the victim. DNA profiles provide a high probability of identity and allow investigators to connect suspects to a specific crime.

The DNA Database

Using a DNA profile created from evidence at a crime scene, forensic serologists look for several important types of matches. They check DNA from one crime-scene sample against the DNA of all other samples from the same crime scene, for instance, to see how many different individuals left their DNA at the scene. Serologists also may compare a DNA profile from one crime scene to profiles taken at another crime scene. A match between DNA profiles from two different crimes could prove that the same suspect was present at both, as in the case of serial rapes and murders.

A DNA profile is most useful when it can be matched to the DNA of a known person, either someone who is already a suspect in the case or someone whose DNA the police already have on file. Since 1998, police departments across the United States have kept a database of the DNA profiles of all people who have been convicted of violent crimes. The database is called the Combined DNA Index System (CODIS), and it is used to match DNA profiles of unidentified suspects to the names of known criminals whose profiles are in the database.

Butler says the process of narrowing down the right person in the database is similar to the way the post office delivers mail. "The entire United States has over 290 million individuals," he says, "but by including the zip code, state, city, street, street number, and name on an envelope, a letter can be delivered to a single, unique individual."[67] Similarly, when the database knows enough of the details and the location markers from one person's DNA, it can track down that precise individual out of millions of possible suspects. When a match is found between two pieces of DNA, the odds that the two DNA samples did *not* come from the same person are less than one in one trillion, making DNA a leading method for identifying perpetrators and for creating an important trail of evidence linking criminals to their victims and the scenes of their crimes.

DNA also is proving useful for identifying victims, especially in cases where the bodies of many victims need to be named. DNA is an important tool in the analysis of scenes of massive crimes such as the September 11, 2001, terrorist attack on the World Trade Center that put investigators to the task of identifying the remains of thousands of individuals. Terrorist attacks, in fact, are becoming an increasing concern in forensic science, not just for serologists, but for experts across the field of forensic biology. Together, forensic biologists are facing the new challenge of predicting how and where bioterrorists may attack—and finding ways to thwart such an attack before people get hurt or killed.

CHAPTER 5

Identifying Microscopic Weapons

A growing field within forensic science focuses on the study of microscopic organisms that could be used to commit crimes. This branch of forensic biology is called microbial forensics, and it studies bacteria, viruses, and biological poisons that could be used as murder weapons. Unlike guns, knives, or bombs, these weapons are microscopic, much too small to be seen with the naked eye. In the hands of someone who knows how to find them, grow them, and use them to hurt people, they can be extremely difficult to control, prevent, or even detect as the cause of a crime.

Solving microbiological crimes is a forensic science specialty much different than the investigation of crimes such as burglary, rape, or murder. In microbiological crime, the weapon itself is especially dangerous. It is likely to be a germ or poison with the ability to travel rapidly through society, infecting hundreds, thousands, even millions of people before it is identified and isolated. The suspect could be a single person, a group of people, or an entire army or national government. The motive may not be personal but a political disagreement between groups or countries.

If the criminals who intentionally released the germ are not tracked down and stopped, they could continue to hurt countless victims. These are the stakes faced by the forensic microbiologists called on to investigate suspicious outbreaks of dangerous illnesses. These experts use their knowledge of biological agents to identify, contain, and prevent crimes of bioterrorism.

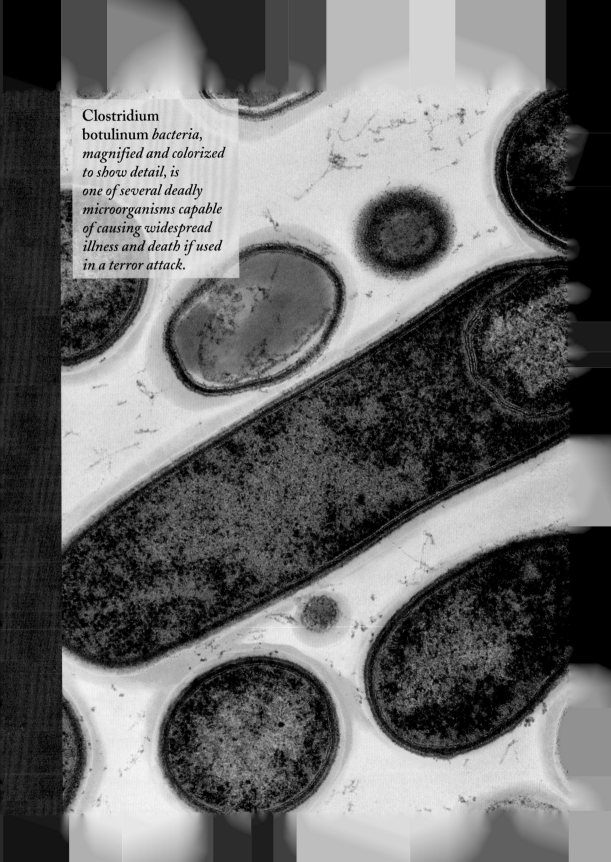

Clostridium botulinum *bacteria, magnified and colorized to show detail, is one of several deadly microorganisms capable of causing widespread illness and death if used in a terror attack.*

Terrorism in Tokyo

The huge threat that biological weapons pose to modern society was demonstrated on the morning of March 20, 1995, in the city of Tokyo when five men stepped onto separate cars of a crowded subway, deposited newspaper-wrapped packages on the floor, pierced the packages with sharpened umbrella handles, and quietly slipped off the train. Within moments, subway passengers began to cough, choke, vomit, and have convulsions. Twelve of the subway commuters died and more than five thousand were injured in one of the world's worst acts of terrorism using a chemical or biological weapon.

Medical personnel tend to victims of a nerve gas attack on a Tokyo subway by the Aum Shinrikyo cult in March 1995.

The substance used on the Tokyo subway was sarin, a poison that can kill a person within ten minutes after it is inhaled. The five men who dispersed the sarin belonged to a powerful Japanese terrorist organization called Aum Shinrikyo, a group that had used chemical and biological weapons in

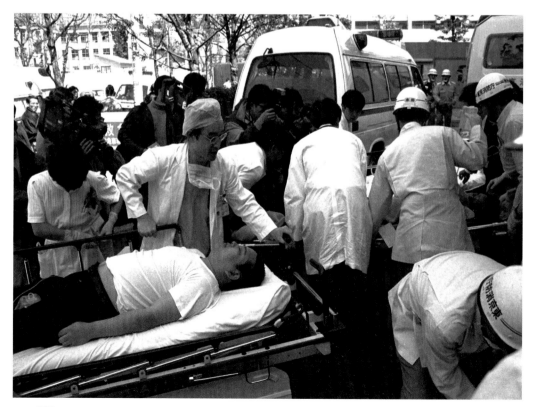

Murder by Virus

In the spring of 1994, a court case made history when it proved that a virus's DNA can show a connection between two infected people. The case involved Richard Schmidt, a doctor in Lafayette, Indiana, whose girlfriend claimed he had injected her with a syringe of blood drawn from a patient who had human immunodeficiency virus (HIV). Six months later, Schmidt's girlfriend was HIV positive, and Schmidt was on trial for attempted murder. Samples of the HIV virus drawn from Schmidt's girlfriend were genetically compared to samples from his HIV-positive patient. Because HIV is a virus that mutates rapidly, there are many different strains of it. But the DNA of the girlfriend's strain was shown to be very similar to the strain carried by Schmidt's

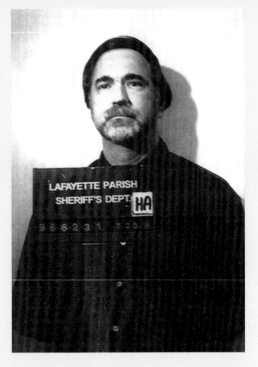

Dr. Richard J. Schmidt is shown in a mug shot taken after his arrest for the attempted murder of his girlfriend whom he injected with HIV. He was convicted in 1998 and sentenced to fifty years in prison.

patient. Neither strain was similar to other known strains in the Lafayette area. Thus, the jury concluded that Schmidt had indeed injected his girlfriend with HIV from his patient. Schmidt was convicted of attempted murder and sentenced to fifty years in prison. The case marked the first time that viral mutations were used as evidence in a court case in the United States.

terrorist attacks before. In the early 1990s Aum Shinrikyo used truck-mounted sprayers to dispense a solution of the deadly bacteria *Clostridium botulinum*, which produces the paralyzing toxin that causes botulism, in an area of Tokyo near Japan's Parliament building. Soon after this attempted botulism attack, Aum Shinrikyo dispersed airborne *Bacillus anthracis*, the bacteria that causes anthrax poisoning, over a Japanese crowd.

When the Japanese government raided Aum Shinrikyo's facilities after the 1995 subway attacks, it found more than two hundred deadly substances and the equipment needed to spread them. "The cult had made several attempts at creating and spreading such biological agents," says Erica Simons, senior writer for the American College of Forensic Examiners. "It is estimated that millions of people could have been killed if these items had been successfully used in terrorist attacks."[68]

At the time of the 1995 Tokyo subway incident, Aum Shinrikyo also had facilities in the United States—one located just a few blocks from Times Square in New York City. The clear necessity of preventing bioterrorism incidents on American soil led the United States government to develop a strong approach to fighting bioterror. This approach relies on the expertise of microbiologists who are familiar with the major biological weapons that exist. They understand the symptoms these germs or poisons cause in the human population and can determine which of these substances are most likely to be used as weapons in crime, as well as identify dangerous individuals or organizations that could have access to them.

Detecting the Crime

"The potential of biological weapons being used is greater than at any other time in history,"[69] say microbiologists Bruce Budowle and colleagues. "Detection and identification are keys to thwart bioterrorism."[70] Knowing what germs and poisons exist is the first step in solving a deliberate, criminal outbreak of infectious disease. Scientists must identify the biological agent that was used before they can protect the public from infection or track down the source of the weapon.

Because biological weapons are natural, living organisms or the toxins released from these organisms, differentiating a deliberate outbreak from a natural or accidental one is critical to determining whether a crime has occurred. Some of the diseases caused by organisms classified as potential biological weapons also occur naturally from time to time. There are more than one hundred cases of food poisoning from botulism in the United States each year, for example, and these occur because the bacteria that cause botulism live in soil. Families or small farms that improperly preserve their homegrown produce may unintentionally ingest the toxin. Overreacting to an accidental outbreak of an illness such as botulism could not only launch an expensive, unnecessary investigation, it also could cause widespread public panic if people hear that their society might be under a biological attack.

When multiple people in a community come down with serious medical symptoms, a forensic microbiologist evaluates the situation to determine if there is cause to suspect that a bioterror crime has taken place. The microbiologist examines evidence from infected individuals to decide if the outbreak is a suspicious one—a case of disease that occurs in an unexpected place, at an unexpected time of the year, or in a group of people who are not normally at risk for catching the illness. "A naturally occurring disease that is found outside its typical environment may raise suspicion and initiate a forensic investigation,"[71] explain Budowle and his colleagues—for example, an outbreak of botulism in an inner-city neighborhood where nobody grows and cans their own vegetables could be a sign that someone deliberately infected a local food source with botulism. An investigation is launched to identify the

> **By the Numbers**
>
> **50%**
>
> **Percentage of people who contract botulism who will die if it goes untreated.**

source of a suspicious outbreak. If a forensic microbiologist determines the illness was intentionally caused, police and scientific investigators must act quickly to solve the crime. They have limited time to catch the perpetrators before they infect more people.

Containing a Suspicious Outbreak

It is important to correctly identify the pathogen, or disease-producing agent, used in a suspicious outbreak so that the people who are infected can be treated and the spread of the illness can be contained. "Hundreds of potential pathogens and toxins exist,"[72] say Budowle and his colleagues, but not all of these are equally dangerous to people or equally likely to be used as biological weapons. The toxins that forensic microbiologists consider most dangerous are those that have the greatest potential as weapons: they are easy to cultivate (grow), they survive well in the environment, and they are easy to spread.

The deadliest organisms do not always make the best weapons because they may be hard to grow or to disseminate (spread). An organism that dies as soon as it reaches open air, for instance, would not be effective if solutions of it were sprayed over a crowd. On the other hand, say Budowle and his colleagues, "an organism with limited destructive potential may be readily available and easy to disseminate."[73] Criminals might even prefer a less deadly biological weapon if it can be spread more easily and make more people sick.

Regardless of the pathogen that has been used, once forensic microbiologists identify the cause of an outbreak, they must alert the public so that people can protect themselves with any effective medications and vaccines that are available. "Most health professionals would stress the need for adequate public health preparedness,"[74] says microbiologist Roger G. Breeze. This preparedness can only occur if a forensic microbiologist correctly identifies a suspicious outbreak of a dangerous pathogen.

When faced with thousands of microscopic weapons to consider during a suspicious outbreak, forensic microbiologists narrow down the list by ruling out potential pathogens. The most dangerous biological agents are the ones they hope to eliminate first. These deadly germs have been placed into a special category by the Centers for Disease Control and Prevention (CDC), the foremost public health agency in the United States. They are called Class A agents, and, of all known biological weapons, they have the most potential to do harm. Class A agents cause death or severe injury to people infected with them, and they may be illnesses for which there is no effective treatment. If a Class A agent is released into the public, it could do vast damage to society.

If forensic microbiologists determine that a Class A agent was used as a weapon, the case is given the highest possible

Terror in the Hospital

One of the most frightening infectious diseases on the CDC's Class A list is caused by the Ebola virus, a highly contagious germ that causes fever, sore throat, diarrhea, and vomiting. There is no medication or treatment for Ebola, and although some of its victims get better, many die. The Ebola virus passes easily from one person to another through contact with blood and other body fluids, and scientists believe the virus also has the capability to be airborne. When a person who is sick with Ebola is admitted to a hospital, the illness can spread rapidly to other patients and to healthcare professionals if steps are not taken to prevent any contact with infected body fluids. To date, the major outbreaks of Ebola have happened in Africa. There have been no known cases in the United States. But because there is no cure and scientists are not even sure where Ebola comes from or how the first victim of a new outbreak comes down with the illness, Ebola remains one of the most frightening viruses on the list of major bioterror threats.

public priority. The sooner the culprits are caught and stopped and the sooner people are aware of the danger, the fewer lives will be threatened. Class A illnesses can spread quickly, so every minute of the investigation counts.

Agents with a Criminal History

For decades, microbiologists have been wary of Class A agents, some of which have been used in biological attacks before. Two of the agents used by the terrorist group Aum Shinrikyo in Tokyo in the 1990s, for example, were the Class A bacteria that cause anthrax and botulism, which are among the most dangerous illnesses known to humans. Forensic microbiologists are well aware of the potential these two bacterial organisms have to do harm. "Talk of these infections is on many lips," says Breeze, "and the funds available [to study them] have mushroomed."[75]

The danger of Class A agent *Bacillus anthracis* received national attention in 2001, when almost two dozen people

A chemistry student holds a sample of Bacillus anthracis, *or anthrax bacteria, a dangerous microorganism that creates airborne spores that cause infection if breathed into the lungs.*

in the United States were deliberately infected with anthrax. *Bacillus anthracis* is a spore-forming bacterium—its cells go into a dormant or sleeping stage and become spores that spread easily in the air. If a person breathes in the spores, the bacteria become active again in the lungs. The person then has inhalation anthrax. Twenty-two people got anthrax poisoning in 2001 when spores of anthrax were spread on pieces of mail that passed through the U.S. postal system.

Inhalation anthrax can often be treated with antibiotics, but treatment is most effective if people recognize symptoms in time to receive medication immediately—within twenty-four hours of exposure. The symptoms of anthrax—fever, fatigue, and difficulty breathing—are so similar to influenza that people may not realize they have been infected by a deadly germ until it is too late for medical treatment to save their lives. Five of the Americans infected with anthrax in 2001 died, proving the importance of recognizing symptoms of a bioterror threat as the first step in launching a forensic investigation.

Although very deadly, anthrax is not the worst of the Class A illnesses, in part because anthrax spores are not communicable—they do not spread from one infected person to another. A mother who inhales anthrax, for instance, cannot pass the illness to the rest of her family. This is a property reserved for the most dangerous Class A illnesses of all: communicable, airborne diseases whose germs *do* spread among people who breathe the same air. Such diseases can move through a population as easily and quickly as the common cold, with one important difference: they are deadly.

Communicable Class A germs are the ones bioterrorists covet and the ones forensic investigators fear the most because they are the ones likely to infect the most people and cause the most damage to society. If a germ such as this were used as a criminal weapon, it could potentially affect the world's entire population. One such biological weapon would be smallpox—an illness whose release forensic microbiologists have been well trained to recognize and dread.

Smallpox: A Large Forensic Threat

Smallpox is a serious, often deadly disease in humans. The only known samples of the Variola virus, which causes the illness, have been locked up in high-security research facilities for decades, so the appearance of smallpox in a public outbreak would automatically be suspicious and would indicate bioterror activity. The appearance of smallpox would launch an immediate, intense, and multinational forensic investigation. The death toll of this disease, worldwide, could be catastrophic.

Sores cover the body of a man with smallpox, which has since been eradicated worldwide by vaccination programs.

Smallpox begins with a very high fever and then causes bumps all over the body, which in turn become open sores that leak fluid and form scabs. When the scabs eventually fall off, smallpox is over—but about 30 percent of people who catch the disease do not survive the high fever it causes. The skin of

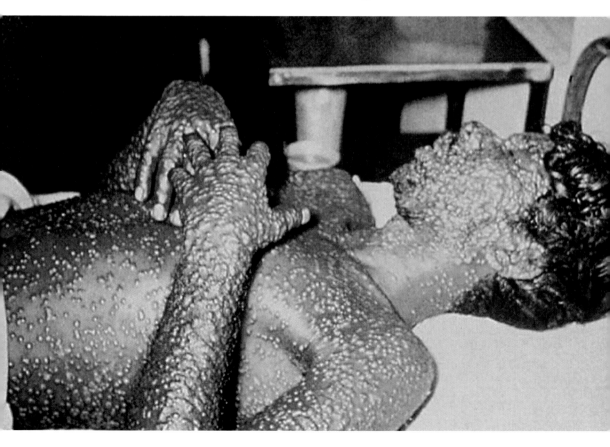

victims who do live is scarred for life by the deep sores.

One reason smallpox is such a concern among forensic microbiologists is that almost no one on earth is immune to it. In the first half of the twentieth century, a smallpox vaccine was created, and a worldwide vaccination program eventually wiped out the illness. Since the year 1949, nobody in the United States has caught smallpox, and since 1977, not a single known case has occurred anywhere in the world. Therefore, for generations, there has been no need to give people the shot that protects against smallpox. But the Variola virus, the cause of the disease, is not totally extinct. There are two remaining samples—one held by the CDC in the United States and the other in a secure biomedical facility in Russia. If a sample of this virus were ever to fall into the hands of a biological criminal, it could again unleash smallpox on civilization.

> **By the Numbers**
>
> # 2 TO 3 DAYS
>
> **Window of time after infection with smallpox virus in which treatment will be effective.**

"An attack with the smallpox virus on the United States would threaten the entire world," says Breeze. "[It] could result in tens of millions of deaths, and could paralyze the economies of industrialized nations."[76] Because the Variola virus is airborne and passes easily from one person to another, Breeze says smallpox "most probably could not today be limited to one country or continent after deliberate release."[77] It is, he says, the most threatening biological weapon among all the Class A agents known by the CDC.

The threat posed by biological agents such as smallpox and anthrax is the focus of a forensic microbiologist's work. Investigations surrounding these deadly substances are further complicated because most illnesses have an incubation period, or a length of time that passes between infection with the germ and the first symptoms it causes. Criminals, therefore, may have several days to hide from the law between the time they dispense the germ and the first symptoms appear in the victims. To combat these challenges, forensic microbiologists are developing new and better methods for investigating criminal outbreaks and bringing to justice the people who cause them. One of the best tools at their disposal is shared information about where infectious agents are kept.

Knowledge Is Power

When investigators discover an outbreak of a suspicious disease and determine that it is the result of a crime, they immediately create a list of places where the criminal or terrorist group could have obtained the germ or toxin. The CDC and organizations like it throughout the world keep careful records of all known viruses, bacteria, and funguses that could be used as weapons in terrorist attacks or biological warfare, including where samples of these agents are kept. Because they track all the laboratories and facilities where dangerous germs or toxins are stored and all the people who have access to them, scientists know that any person or people responsible for releasing this illness on society must be connected in some way to one of those facilities. National information banks such as the U.S. Department of Energy's National Bioforensic Evidence Database improve coordination among investigators who respond to potential uses of biological weapons. Such databases are critical to forensic microbiology, say Budowle and his colleagues, because they keep track of individuals who have access to dangerous pathogens "so that threats can be deterred or traced back effectively to possible sources."[78]

The databases also are a way to keep track of different varieties of bacteria or viruses. An important property of these microbes is that they can mutate—their DNA can change slightly to give them new properties and abilities, such as immunity to a medication or the ability to become airborne. Whenever a bacterium or virus mutates, laboratories that possess the new strain of it keep records of its new DNA. In the event of an outbreak, a forensic microbiologist can examine

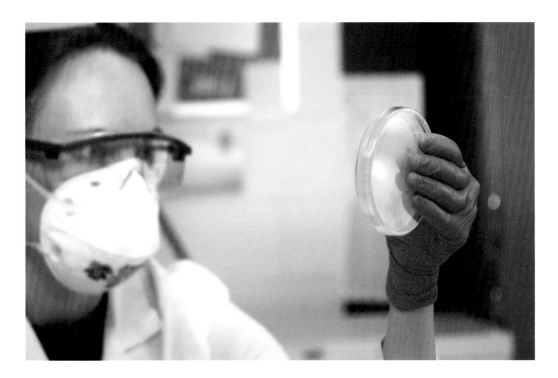

the DNA of the bacteria or virus that is making people sick, determine what strain it is, and then track down the known laboratories that possess that strain of the germ. This pinpoints laboratories where the criminal could have obtained a sample of the dangerous agent.

A scientist examines a sample of bacteria, the characteristics of which are tracked in databases managed by the Centers for Disease Control and other agencies to help identify the source of outbreaks.

Although records of different strains of germs are very useful, a forensic microbiologist is not always able to trace a mutated form of a bacterium or virus to any laboratory source. Bioterrorists who have a strong background in microbiology could deliberately mutate a strain of bacteria or a virus to give it new and unfamiliar properties. Not only could this mutated version be an even more dangerous biological weapon, its new DNA would be impossible to trace back to any known laboratory. Without knowing where the original sample of the organism came from, forensic investigators could have few leads in the case.

The DNA altering, called genetic engineering, that bioterrorists may use to make infectious agents more deadly also could benefit forensic microbiologists. They use genetic engineering themselves to solve cases of biological crime more quickly. Microbiologists can insert new material into the DNA of certain viruses or bacteria, and these new series of genes serve as an identity tag that will be passed down to all future generations of that particular germ, even if it is later mutated further by a criminal scientist. Inserting a different DNA tag for the germ at each laboratory that carries it allows forensic microbiologists to keep detailed records of these organisms and the laboratories that possess them.

Infectious disease specialist Nancy Khardori says these identification tags make "genetic fingerprinting" of microbial agents possible. During a suspicious outbreak of an illness, a forensic microbiologist can now examine the DNA of the bacteria or virus, looking for a genetically engineered tag. If a tag is present, the microbiologist knows that the germ was stolen and can trace it back to the specific laboratory it came from. The culprit will likely be someone with a connection to that laboratory, which will help investigators come up with a list of suspects in the crime. As this genetic technology is perfected, says Khardori, it "will enhance our capability to detect, trace, and manage bioterrorism events,"[79] making it harder for criminals to get away with microbiological crime.

Powerful Prevention for Global Crime

Most branches of forensic biology react to crimes that have already happened. Botanists find answers to questions about where a crime took place, and taphonomists try to determine how long it has been since a murder occurred. Anthropologists and odontologists analyze a victim's bones and teeth to figure out a dead person's identity, and serologists use body fluids to prove a link between suspects, victims, and crime scenes.

Forensic microbiology, unlike most other biological branches of forensic science, tries to solve crimes that are committed invisibly with biological weapons that are too small to see. The crime scene itself—the exact place where the victims are infected—may never be known. But by tracking down missing or stolen germs and tracing infectious agents back to the places they came from, forensic microbiologists work to identify the people spreading these biological agents and stop them before they do more damage.

The stakes are higher for the forensic microbiologist than in any other branch of forensic biology. As gatekeepers, these experts are faced with the crucial task of identifying crimes that have the potential to have an impact on the security of a nation and even the entire world. Like all forensic biologists, these scientists use their knowledge of life to protect it.

Notes

Chapter 1: A Trail of Plant Evidence

1. Heather Mill Coyle, Cheng-Lung Lee, Wen-Yu Lin, Henry C. Lee, and Timothy M. Palmbach, "Using plant evidence to aid in forensic death investigation," *Croatian Medical Journal* 246 (2005): pp. 606–12, 607.

2. David W. Hall, "Forensic Botany," in *Forensic Taphonomy*, edited by William D. Haglund and Marcella H. Sorg. Boca Raton, FL: CRC Press, 1996, p. 353.

3. Coyle et al., "Using plant evidence," p. 609.

4. Coyle et al., "Using plant evidence," p. 610.

5. Heather Mill Coyle, *Forensic Botany*. Boca Raton, FL: CRC Press, 2004, p. 251.

6. Coyle, *Forensic Botany*, p. 251.

7. Vernon G. Geberth, *Practical Homicide Investigation*. Boca Raton, FL: CRC Press, 2006, p. 250.

8. Geberth, *Practical Homicide Investigation*, p. 99.

9. Geberth, *Practical Homicide Investigation*, p. 99.

10. Geberth, *Practical Homicide Investigation*, p. 250.

11. Coyle et al., "Using plant evidence," p. 611.

Chapter 2: Death's Timeline

12. Arpad A. Vass, "Beyond the Grave—Understanding Human Decomposition," *Microbiology Today*, November 2001, p. 192.

13. Vass, "Beyond the Grave," pp. 190–91.

14. Colin Evans, *Murder Two: The Second Casebook of Forensic Investigation*. Hoboken, NJ: John Wiley & Sons, 2004, p. 268.

15. Evans, *Murder Two*, p. 269.

16. Evans, *Murder Two*, p. 269.

17. Evans, *Murder Two*, p. 269.

18. Jessica Snyder Sachs, *Corpse: Nature, Forensics, and the Struggle to Pinpoint Time of Death*. Cambridge, MA: Perseus Books, 2001, p. 21.

19. Vincent J. DiMaio and Dominick DiMaio, *Forensic Pathology*, 2nd ed. Boca Raton, FL: CRC Press, 2001, p. 31.

20. Sachs, *Corpse*, p. 21.

21. Sachs, *Corpse*, p. 21.

22. Sachs, *Corpse*, p. 70.

23. DiMaio and DiMaio, *Forensic Pathology*, p. 39.

24. DiMaio and DiMaio, *Forensic Pathology*, p. 40.

25. DiMaio and DiMaio, *Forensic Pathology*, p. 40.

26. Jay Dix and Michael A. Graham, *Time of Death, Decomposition, and Identification: An Atlas*. Boca Raton, FL: CRC Press, 2000,, p. 9.

27. Dix and Graham, *Time of Death*, p. 9.

28. DiMaio and DiMaio, *Forensic Pathology*, p. 39.

29. DiMaio and DiMaio, *Forensic Pathology*, p. 40.

30. Evans, *Murder Two*, p. 76.

31. Sachs, *Corpse*, p. 79.

Chapter 3: Reading the Bones

32. Richard H. Walton, *Cold Case Homicides*. Boca Raton, FL: CRC Press, 2006, p. 379.

33. Stanley Rhine, *Bone Voyage: A Journey in Forensic Anthropology*. Albuquerque: University of New Mexico Press, 1998, p. 50.

34. Rhine, *Bone Voyage*, p. 26.

35. Rhine, *Bone Voyage*, p. 50.

36. Walton, *Cold Case Homicides*, p. 371.

37. Louise Scheuer and Sue Black, "Osteology," in *Forensic Human Identification: An Introduction*, edited by Tim Thompson and Sue Black. Boca Raton, FL: CRC Press, 2006, p. 200.

38. Rhine, *Bone Voyage*, p. 16.

39. J. R. Gaur, "Identification of Human Skeletons," in *Recent Advances in Forensic Biology*, edited by A. K. Guru and Pankaj Shrivastava. New Delhi, India: Anmol Publications, 2002, p. 4.

40. Walton, *Cold Case Homicides*, p. 371.

41. Scheuer and Black, "Osteology," p. 214.

42. Scheuer and Black, "Osteology," p. 216.

43. Rhine, *Bone Voyage*, p. 91.

44. Scheuer and Black, "Osteology," p. 213.

45. Sachs, *Corpse*, p. 52.

46. Sachs, *Corpse*, p. 52.

47. Rhine, *Bone Voyage*, p. 63.

48. Scheuer and Black, "Osteology," p. 202.

49. James H. Hardy, "Odontology," in *Forensic Human Identification: An Introduction*, edited by Tim Thompson and Sue Black. Boca Raton, FL: CRC Press, 2006, p. 178.

50. Hardy, "Odontology," p. 185.

51. Hardy, "Odontology," p. 185.

52. Hardy, "Odontology," p. 178.

Chapter 4: Body Fluids Left Behind

53. Katherine Ramsland, "Serology: It's in the Blood." *TruTV*. www.trutv.com/library/crime/criminal_mind/forensics/serology/3.html.

54. Joe Nickell and John F. Fischer, *Crime Science*. Lexington: University Press of Kentucky, 1999, p. 195.

55. Nickell and Fischer, *Crime Science*, p. 196.

56. Colin Wilson and Damon Wilson, *Written in Blood: A History of Forensic Detection*. New York: Carroll & Graf, 2003, p. 257.

57. Colin Evans, *The Casebook of Forensic Detection*. New York: John Wiley & Sons, 1996, p. 202.

58. Wilson and Wilson, *Written in Blood*, p. 255.

59. Wilson and Wilson, *Written in Blood*, p. 255.

60. Nickell and Fischer, *Crime Science*, p. 195.

61. Nickell and Fischer, *Crime Science*, p. 195.

62. John M. Butler, *Forensic DNA Typing: Biology, Technology, and Genetics of STR Markers*, 2nd ed. Burlington, MA: Academic Press, 2005, p. 17.

63. Butler, *Forensic DNA Typing*, p. 5.

64. Rosalind Bowman, Teri J. Labbe, and Kimberly A. Mullings, "Serology and DNA Evidence," in *Forensic Emergency Medicine*, 2nd ed., edited by Jonathan Olshaker, M. Christine Jackson, and William S. Smock. Philadelphia, PA: Lippincott, Williams & Wilkins, 2006, p. 237.

65. Butler, *Forensic DNA Typing*, p. 4.

66. Butler, *Forensic DNA Typing*, p. 4.

67. Butler, *Forensic DNA Typing*, p. 4.

Chapter 5: Identifying Microscopic Weapons

68. Erica Simons, "Faith, Fanatacism, and Fear: Aum Shinrikyo—The Birth and Death of a Terrorist Organization," *The Forensic Examiner*, Spring 2006, pp. 37–45.

69. Bruce Budowle, Mark R. Wilson, James P. Burans, Roger B. Breeze, and Ranajit Chakraborty, "Microbial Forensics," in *Microbial Forensics*, edited by Roger Breeze, Bruce Budowle, and Steven E. Schutzer. San Diego, CA: Academic Press, 2005, p. 8.

70. Budowle et al., "Microbial Forensics," p. 10.

71. Budowle et al., "Microbial Forensics," p. 16.

72. Budowle et al., "Microbial Forensics," p. 14.

73. Budowle et al., "Microbial Forensics," p. 14.

74. Roger E. Breeze, "Infectious Disease: Not Just a Health Matter Anymore," in *Microbial Forensics*, edited by Roger Breeze, Bruce Budowle, and Steven E. Schutzer. San Diego, CA: Academic Press, 2005, p. 30.

75. Breeze, "Infectious Disease," p. 27.

76. Breeze, "Infectious Disease," p. 30.

77. Breeze, "Infectious Disease," p. 29.

78. Budowle et al., "Microbial Forensics," p. 10.

79. Nancy Khardori, ed., *Bioterrorism Preparedness*. Weinheim, Germany: Wiley-VCH, 2006, p. xii.

Glossary

adenosine triphosphate (ATP): A substance produced by the body's cells to give them energy.

airborne: capable of being spread by air; especially, a germ that can be passed by breathing infected air.

anthrax: an infectious disease caused by the bacterium *Bacillus anthracis*.

antibiotic: a medication used to kill bacteria that have infected the body.

bioterrorism: terrorism using biological weapons such as contagious diseases.

blood type: one of four different types of human blood that are differentiated by proteins on the surfaces of blood cells; can be A, B, AB, or O.

botulism: an infectious disease caused by the bacterium *Clostridium botulinum*.

cartilage: soft, elastic tissue that composes the ends of certain bones in juveniles and is replaced by bone tissue at maturity.

chemiluminescence: the process by which certain chemical reactions give off a glow.

Class A Agent: a category of infectious illnesses designated as the most dangerous to people, especially as a bioterrorism threat.

Combined DNA Index System (CODIS): a database of the DNA profiles of known criminals in the United States.

deoxyribonucleic acid (DNA): the two-strand molecule in every living cell that contains the genetic material the cell needs to survive and reproduce.

epiphyses: the rounded end of a long bone.

exhume: to remove or dig up a buried body.

forensic anthropologist: a scientist who studies human remains to determine characteristics that may be helpful in their identification.

forensic entomologist: a scientist who studies the insects that colonize corpses during decomposition.

forensic odontologist: an expert who identifies human remains by matching their teeth to dental records of a known missing person.

hemoglobin: a protein found in red blood cells that binds oxygen molecules to iron so the oxygen can be carried to the body's tissues.

incubation period: the length of time between being infected with a pathogen and showing symptoms of illness.

individuation: the process of singling out one individual from every other.

Kastle-Meyer Color Test: a test performed on evidence to determine whether a substance is blood.

livor mortis: the process by which blood sinks and pools at the point of lowest gravity in a dead body.

luminol: a chemical compound that gives off a faint blue light when it comes into contact with the iron in blood.

metamorphosis: the process by which certain organisms, such as many insects, undergo drastic physical changes as they mature into adults.

microbial forensics: the branch of forensic science that focuses on identifying, solving, and preventing crimes of bioterrorism.

phenolphthalein: a chemical compound that turns bright pink in the presence of blood.

precipitin test: a test that combines a trace of blood with rabbit serum to look for a cloudy precipitin that indicates the blood is human.

putrefaction: the decomposition of organic matter, including human bodies.

rigor mortis: the process by which the body's muscles become stiff and rigid after death.

serology: the study and analysis of body fluids.

serum: the liquid portion of an animal fluid, such as blood.

smallpox: a disease caused by the Variola virus whose symptoms include fever and seeping sores on the skin.

taphonomy: the study of how human remains decompose.

toxin: a poisonous or disease-causing substance.

For More Information

Books

Anna Prokos. 2007. *Guilty by a Hair! Real-Life DNA Matches*. New York: Franklin Watts. Cases of criminals caught by the DNA they left at the crime scene are detailed in this book.

Peggy Thomas. 2008. *Talking Bones: The Science of Forensic Anthropology*. New York: Facts on File . This book discusses historical and modern uses of forensic anthropology and how it has solved criminal cases. Diagrams and photographs illustrate the featured concepts.

Articles

Martin Enserink, and Yudhijit Bhattacharjee. August 8, 2008. "Bioterrorism: Scientists Seek Answers, Ponder Future after Anthrax Case Suicide." *Science Magazine* 321: 754–755. The article discusses the anthrax terrorism incident of 2001 and what it means for the nation's response to bioterror threats in the future.

Vaughn M. Bryant, Jr. and Dallas C. Mildenhall. "Forensic Palynology: A New Way to Catch Crooks." *Crimes and Clues*. http://www.crimeandclues.com/pollen.htm (accessed January 23, 2009). This online article discusses palynology, the study of plant pollen and how it can be used as evidence to help solve crimes.

Web Sites

Botanical Society of America. "Plant Talking Point." *BSA's Classroom*. www.botany.org/PlantTalkingPoints/crime.php. Case studies of some of the most interesting crimes botany has helped to solve are described on this Web page, as well as the techniques scientists used to crack them.

ConceptCreators, Inc. "Skeletal System—Anatomy and Physiology." *Get Body Smart*. www.getbodysmart.com/ap/skeletalsystem/skeleton/menu/animation.html. Practice with this online tutorial and learn what forensic anthropologists must know to put bones from crime scenes back together into skeletons. Descriptions, diagrams, and real-life photographs create a fun tutorial for learning each of the body's 206 bones.

Discovery Communications, LLC. "How DNA Evidence Works." *How Stuff Works*. www.howstuffworks.com/dna-evidence.htm. Pictures and diagrams accompany this explanation of what DNA is, how two samples are compared to one another, and how DNA is used in forensic investigations. Links to interactive DNA evidence quizzes make this new knowledge fun.

Centers for Disease Control and Prevention. "Bioterrorism Agents/Diseases." *Emergency Preparedness and Response.* www.bt.cdc.gov/Agent/Agentlist.asp.

Use this A to Z listing of bioterrorism threats and diseases to look up anthrax, Ebola, smallpox, and more. There are additional links to information on bioterrorism and what the CDC, and individuals, can do.

Index

Picture Credits

Cover Photo: Raul Arboleda/AFP/Getty Images
AFP/Getty Images, 63
AJP/Hop Américain/Photo Researchers, Inc., 65
AP Images, 22, 42, 76, 77, 82
CAMR/A. Barry Dowsett/Photo Researchers, Inc., 75
E.R. Degginger/Photo Researchers, Inc., 39
Getty Images, 84
Hulton Archive/Getty Images, 19
iStockPhoto.com/Awakened Eye, 18
iStock Photo.com/Chemicalbilly, 87
iStockPhoto.com/EyeJoy, 20
iStockPhoto.com/gmutlu, 53
iStockPhoto.com/Tomasz Szymanski, 9
Jerome Wexler/Photo Researchers, Inc., 13
Joe Raedle/Getty Images, 58
John Bartholomew/Corbis, 29
JOHN SOMMERS/Reuters/Corbis, 50
Martin Shields/Photo Researchers, Inc., 71
Mauro Fermariello/Photo Researchers, Inc., 26
Peter Menzel/Photo Researchers, Inc., 46
Philippe Psaila/Photo Researchers, Inc., 36, 59
Russell Kightley/Photo Researchers, Inc., 47
Steve Gschmeissner/Photo Researchers, Inc., 32
Tek Image/Photo Researchers, Inc., 68
VideoSurgery/Photo Researchers, Inc., 48
Volker Steger/Photo Researchers, Inc., 27

About the Author

Jenny MacKay is an editor of books and journal articles and the author of several nonfiction books for teens, including *Fingerprints and Impression Evidence*. She is currently pursuing her MFA degree in creative writing. She lives with her husband and two children in northern Nevada, where she was born and raised.